A FRIGHTENED RABBIT PUBLICATION

THE WORK

The lyrics of Scott Hutchison

FABER *ff* MUSIC

CONTENTS

"A FRIGHTENED RABBIT EP"

"STATE HOSPITAL EP"

"PEDESTRIAN VERSE"

"PAINTING OF A PANIC ATTACK"

"RECORDED SONGS"

FOREWORD

"I haven't quite found the right word for what it is,
whether it's therapeutic or cathartic. I love that there
are bits of my life in this little package right here. I
like the mathematical approach. I was asked 'do I write
stories or poems outside of music', and I don't because
the structure of music really appeals to my brain.
The process of finishing songs and putting them in a
neat little place isn't cathartic, it's more like
'OK, I understand that now'."

Scott
2016

Scott spoke a long time ago of wanting to create a
book with DLT, the man who's brought this wonderful
collection to life and worked alongside Scott for the
majority of FR artwork over the years.

This is not exactly the book Scott would've made and
this foreword doesn't seem enough for what is to follow,
but that is OK. We're certain he'd enjoy flicking
through the pages with a shake of the head, a wry smile
and the occasional outburst.

Acknowledging the years in this form without him wasn't
an easy task. We hadn't engaged with the songs in such
a way since his death and doing so brought deep waves
of emotion and meant laugh-crying in the kitchen wasn't
out of the ordinary. To review our collective creativity
and remember the days, challenging each other to push
ourselves and what we thought the band was musically,
was a joy. It feels like a dream. Another lifetime.
Over the Frightened Rabbit years the words were never
really discussed. There was a line in the sand, the
music is the band; the words, Scott.

Reading through the lyrics can bring us to many places,
evenings in the Barrowlands full of pride and joy or
late night on the street filled full of stark despair,
head in hands, ultimately to an altar of regret.
We can't always control where we go, wherever we end up,
we feel the connection to the moments shared, the beauty
and the unpredictability of being part of a band and an
inner connection to ourselves and our finite time.

These words will always bring us into Scott's world,
often with brutal honesty. They are a portal of
connection to him and parts of ourselves. Many of the
songs are Scott sharing his path through life. At times
showing elements of himself he was not proud of and that
vulnerability echoes and shines a light into parts of us
we often find difficult to explore.
Contrast and conflict are constants on the pages,
songs we know Scott was immensely proud of, some he
couldn't tell where they'd come from, springing forth
over minutes, others laboured over years, evolving
slightly before the commitment to tape. One or two we
don't think he cared for too much really, over time not
recognising himself in them or finding something lazy or
uncomfortable within.

Time gives us a chance to reflect and for the songs to
evolve and grow in different ways out in the ether.
We change, and with that the relationships to the
songs evolve.

They will continue to create bonds all over the world
and let us connect with Scott in our own way.

We hope this book allows you that too.

Andy Jilly Grant Simon

REF
618-19207.

ARTIST   FRIGHTENED RABBIT

TITLE   "Sing The Greys"

MONTH / YEAR

JUN 5 2006

NOV 1 9 2007

"THE GREYS"

What's the blues, when you've got the greys?
I think I've given up, my body's given in
in a building I lie still
then I turn back over again
in a building that has heating
sweat, sweat, sweat, sweat dried-on stains.

I'm sick of feeling sick and not throwing up
you sit in my stomach and you seem to be stuck
it won't work its way through my guts and just go away.
I woke up this afternoon thought, maybe today
the world might be a more colourful place
but there's no luck, it's still just grey
come back here.

What's the blues, when you've got the greys?
Much less productive than hardship and pain
in a building I lie still
just before I turn over again
in a building that has heating
sweat, sweat, sweat, sweat dried-on stains.

I'm sick of feeling sick and not throwing up
you sit in my stomach and you seem to be stuck
it won't work its way through my guts and just go away.
I woke up this afternoon thought, maybe today
the world might be a more colourful place
but there's no luck, it's still just grey.

What's the blues when you've got the greys?
I don't have much of a story to say
I just sit around at night and avoid day
if I do anything at all it would be to get up
and avoid conversation and human contact
'cause you can't touch the world if you can't even feel pain
you should come back here.

[redacted] MUSIC! NOW!

~~NOW I KNOW~~
~~YOU ARE ALL WASTING YOUR TIME~~
~~STRONG FEELINGS DON'T COME OFTEN~~
~~SO I'M NOT WASTING MINE.~~

AT 25 I WILL DIE
MY USE BY OH!
I WASN'T PUT IN THE FRIDGE
AND SOON I'LL GROW CULTURES.
HISTORY'S PETRI DISH.

YOU ARE ALL WASTING YOUR TIME.
YOU'VE GOT NO GIVEN RIGHT TO WASTE MINE.
I HAVE PLOUGH! I HAVE HORSES!
THIS FURROW ~~WILL GO DEEP~~ [redacted] AND ROOTS FLOURISH.
CHURNS DEEP

[redacted]

BIG L SMILES AND KISSES MY
CHEEK AND TO MY SURPRISE
KISSES THE OTHER ONE TOO.
~~LOVE NEVER~~ [redacted]
SO THIS NOW WE DO THINGS HERE
LET'S PRETEND THAT WE ARE FLOWERS
LETS PRETEND WE GIVE SOME FUCKS.
WE GIVE SOME FUCKS
WE GIVE SOME FUCKS.

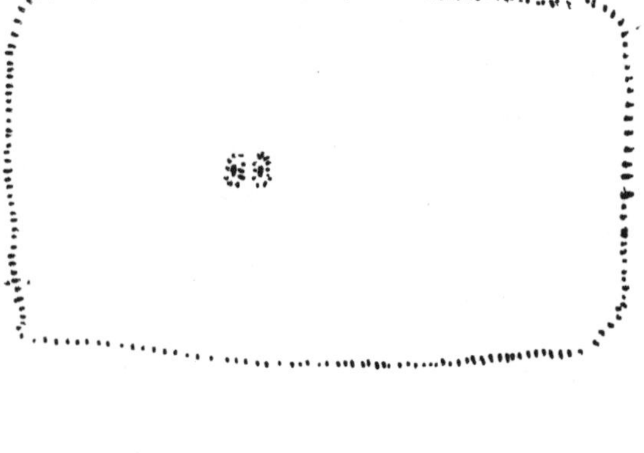

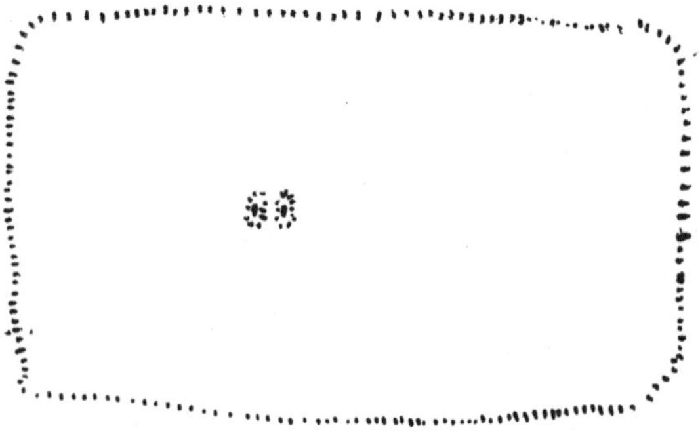

"MUSIC NOW"

Music now is quite amazing
musicians unite against the enemy
writing is a job
making someone look dumb is not.
So if this song falls on deaf ears
I'll lip-synch it so you can hear
I can hum for days and weeks and years
I won't shout nor will I scream
will I scream.

So love me London, love me
or don't love me I don't mind
you can take it or leave
and you'll ignore us
by kissing us on both cheeks
oh know how you work
I'll blush you red on your back
remember me this one time,
'cause I'll never be back
I do not hate this music
I only hate the fucks that
cling on then give it up.

You are all wasting your time here
you've got no right to waste mine as well, my dear
make your music, make it so loud and so trite
make your music, make music that some cunt might like.

Make music now
this is music now.

"Y A W N S"

That infectious wind we breathe
fills up the bored hole that lust leaves.

He yawns
she yawns as well
she yawns because she's bored
he yawns because he can't sleep anymore.

They go out, fill their mouths with drink and food
so they don't have to speak
then in between courses they are gasping for air
so they yawn and look at their feet.

She yawns
he yawns as well
she yawns because she's bored
he yawns because he can't sleep anymore.

He yawns because he's tired
the girl that he slept with sleeps too soon at night
when she yawns, she tells the truth
that the boy she adored is just the man she's contracted to
Girl what of you and me?
Admit that you're bored, you need more electricity
I've had enough of love
it just ends with two yawns in unison.

618-19207/04

SHE YAWNS
HE YAWNS AS WELL
SHE YAWNS BECAUSE SHE'S BORED
HE YAWNS BECAUSE HE CAN'T SLEEP ANYMORE.

I CAN'T REMEMBER LAST YEAR
HUNGER HAS COME TO WREAK TODAY
HE YAWNS
HE YAWNS AS WELL
SHE CAN'T LIE BE IF THEY DON'T SPEAK
IN THE SAME BED.

FEED

FEED   FEED

THIS IS NOT SO NEED A LINE IN THE SAND
I WOULD HOP TO HERE BEFORE THE TIDE COMES IN.

YOU SHOULD BE...

THIS IS ~~ALL~~ I HEAR, YOUR HIGH HORSESHITE
YOU HAVE BEEN MISLEAD YOURHIGH HORSE IS A PONY ~~~~

YOU SHOULD BE... etc.

"BE LESS RUDE"

Oh, this is what we need
a line in the sand
I would cross to here
before the tide comes in.

You should be less rude
you don't know what it might do for you
I'd be less rude to you
and we might just get along, too.

You sit on your high horse
you're spouting high horse SHITE
I'm afraid you've been misled
your high horse, in fact, is a pony.

You should be less rude
you don't know what it might do for you
I'd be less rude to you
and we might just get along, too.

Take that back now, take that back
you should take that back, back, back.

You should be less rude
you don't know what it might do for you
I'd be less rude to you
and we might just get along, too.

"GO-GO GIRLS"

I'd think about light, I'd think about lifting
that brick off your mind, it's making you ill.
I know it's not quite the custom in this country
but if you never try then you'll never know, no you won't.

Therefore, insert a pipe somewhere in your forearm
bleed the vein dry, fill up your bowl.
Head out in a hearse, set up like the circus
seems sinister at first, but there's dancing girls.

It's just me and my brother giving blood on the
street tonight
we are not messiahs, ours is not the blood of Christ
don't wait for a second, what you want might never arrive.

So, so, don't be scared, don't be too shy, to give out your
good blood
drive round town give it out, spilling your guts, love
and you know, tous les choses that you wanted in the
first place
might just come your way in a shape you could not expect.

It's just me and my brother giving blood on the
street tonight
we are not messiahs, ours is not the blood of Christ
don't wait for a second, what you want might never arrive.

It's just me and my brother giving blood on the streets
Go-Go Girls in the back seat yeah they're drinking it neat
are you thirsty like a murderer who's just been released?
You should paint your face red 'cause you're this close
to death
so if it's running in your veins and there's people in
need tonight.

"BEHAVE!"

Okay stab, okay stab
please me I don't care how
stab me and please me now
with your mouth.

A big bad, big bad
ape in a prison room
he's just itching to telephone you
with his mouth.

Behave! Behave!
I don't know quite how to behave.

Patience, patience
leaves me with dross to bear
leaves me, I don't know where
then it leaves me out.

Distance, distance
leaves me, I'm ashamed to say
where I'll make a mess on the stairs
with my mouth.

Behave! Behave!
I don't know quite how to behave.
Behave!
I don't have a clue how to behave when I'm around you ...

Behave around you ...

SQUARE 9

(4)

~~GOOD~~ BIG ~~SEEDS~~ I'D SAY ARE
~~MORE~~ ~~PEER THAN CONCRETE~~
BY DAY COLONISE.
BY NIGHT BRING PEACE.

HEAP SOME ~~OUR~~ HOPES
AND ~~COMPILE A CROONERS~~ WOES
WORK OUT HOW TO
~~FINISH THOUGH~~ COMPLETE.

(CH) PEEL
~~EXCITE~~ THOSE EARS ~~THEY~~
ITS IMPORTANT THAT ~~THEY~~ HEAR
~~HEAD DAILY MAYBE~~
THIS HOPEFUL NICE.

~~CREATE~~ STUB OUT FEAR
THERE'S ~~SOMETHING~~ I LIKE ABOUT THIS YEAR
SQUARE 9 IS HERE.

(4)

BUT CALM! CALM!
IN THE RIBS. ~~~~ I GRAB A HAND
STAGES ARE JUST STAGES FOR US TO
PASS.

PEEL
~~~~ THOSE EARS
ITS IMPORTANT THAT THEY HEAR
THIS HOPEFUL SMILE.
THE LACK OF FEAR
IS WHAT I LIKE ABOUT THIS YEAR.
SQUARE 9 IS HERE.
BACK X IIII

"S Q U A R E   9"

My good big deeds
I'd say are more like plans than concrete
by day we'll colonise
by night, we'll bring peace.

Heap all your hopes
compile a crooner's woes
work out how to, how to complete these.

You can peel those eyes
'cause it's important that they see
my hopeful smile.
Then you stub out fear
there's something I like about this year
Square 9 is here.

So calm, stay calm
right there behind your ribs and grab my hand
stages are just stages for us to pass.

You should peel those ears
'cause it's important that they hear
my hopeful words.
And stub out fear
there's something I like about this year
Square 9 is here, is here.

It'll be like Square 1
where we fell in love
forget about Square 2
it was not me and you
just like Square 1
where we fell in love, under the tree
forget about Square 3
oh, that wasn't me
like Square 1
where we fell in love
forget about Square 5
I was only half alive.

"SNAKE"

~~Me and Snake talk about you every day~~
~~I can't wait to see your face~~
~~he tells me he feels the same.~~

~~We lie awake, we're tired but we can't get to sleep~~
~~I'm tired 'cause I've scraped through the day~~
~~he's tired because he's been out late, again.~~

~~And there he lies, staring up with his big gay eyes~~
~~he whispers to me, 'Aren't you tired?'~~
~~'I'm tired of missing B.'~~

~~I'll wake with Snake~~
~~he's soft inside but not as soft as you~~
~~I love that Snake but I love you more~~
~~and he's no substitute~~
~~I'll wake, I'll wake with you soon.~~

~~Yesterday Snake told me about the time when he~~
~~came to meet you off the plane~~
~~and we all drove home in Wheels.~~

~~He was proud and awfully glad that I took him out~~
~~I said, 'How does New York sound?'~~
~~He said, 'It sounds quite loud.'~~

~~So pack your pipes~~
~~pack your Chapstick and your tights~~
~~and one shoe for going out at night~~
~~we're going to visit B.~~

FUCK OFF

~~We'll take a camera~~
~~and go to the zoo~~
~~and take pictures of other snakes with you~~
~~and hope one of 'em turns out to be gay.~~

~~I'll wake with Snake~~
~~he's soft inside but not as soft as you~~
~~I love that Snake but I love you more~~
~~and he's no substitute~~
~~I'll wake, I'll wake with you soon.~~

REF	618-93192319.
ARTIST	FRIGHTENED RABBIT
TITLE	"It's Christmas So We'll Stop"

MONTH / YEAR

DEC 1 7 2007

DEC 1 5 2008

[ITS CHRISTMAS
[LET THE RUN.
[NOW THE COLD.
[IT IS WARM...
[LIFE MIGHT NEVER

_____

[ITS CHRISTMAS.

[IN FACT FORGET

[AND WHEN YOU ARE TUCKED.

[I'LL PROTECT YOU.

_____

[ITS CHRISTMAS SO WE'LL STOP
WHILE IT NOT FOR.
[AS WE SLEEP BY THE FALL.

IT'S CHRISTMAS
SO WELL STOP

IT'S CHRISTMAS
SO WE'LL STOP

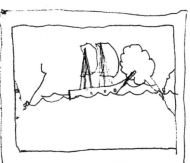

"IT'S CHRISTMAS SO WE'LL STOP"

It's Christmas so we'll stop
it's on with the lights to warm the dark
it can cloak elsewhere
as the rot stops for today

Let the rot stop just for one day
only good red eyes, red suits
and faces will radiate
and the cold will hide its face

Now the cold has turned away
we can be best friends with the people we hate
'cause we've all got blood
and it's warmer than you'd think

Yeah, it is warm and it is thick
we all breathe out clouds
we were built to give at least once each year
and that's better than never I guess

And life might never get better than this
with the perfect excuse for our natures to change
and wear shiny clothes
oh, it's Christmas so press pause on the remote

Oh, it's Christmas so we'll stop
'cause the wine on our breath puts the love in our
tongues so forget the names
I called you on Christmas Eve

In fact, forget the entire year
don't reflect, just pretend and you won't feel scared
you won't feel a thing
'cause it's all been tucked away

And once you're tucked in bed
you'll hug on to the day for the last few seconds
your cradled face,
is protected from the wind

And I'll protect you I promise I will
and the rest of our lives will be just like Christmas
with fewer toys
you're a good girl, I'm a good boy
or so I thought

Oh, it's Christmas so we stopped
were it not for the tick of the clock
and the spin of the Earth in space
we could always be this way

And as we sleep at the fall of the day
in the room next door as the tree lights brighten
the rodent's eye
catches a glimpse of the dust beginning to rise

The next day life went back to its bad self.
The next day life went back to its bad self.
The next day life went back to its bad self.
The next day life went back to its bad self.

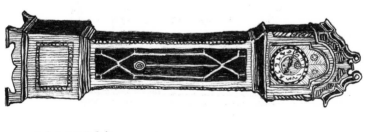

REF

618-2013156.

ARTIST

FRIGHTENED RABBIT

TITLE

"The Midnight Organ Fight"

MONTH / YEAR

APR 1 4 2008

THE MODERN LEPER

~~A CRIPPLE WALKS AMONGST YOU ALL~~

~~YOU TIRED HUMAN BEINGS~~

A CRIPPLE WALKS AMONGST YOU ALL

YOU TIRED HUMAN BEINGS

ITS GOT ~~EVERYTHING~~ A CRIPPLE HAS NOT

TWO WORKING ARMS AND LEGS

BUT CHRIST TURN IT INTO A BIRD, ITS A USELESS HUMAN BEING

YET IT VEGETATES AS A VOLUNTEER

TO WHAT ~~MOOT IN YOU A DUAL~~ FATE

~~PARTS FALL FROM~~ ~~THIS~~ SYSTEM

AND THEY WON'T GROW BACK AGAIN

VITALLY, IT DOESN'T MISS THEM

HE 'IS TOO FAR GONE 'IN TO CARE

IS THAT YOU? THAT IS YOU!

IN FRONT OF ME? ~~IN FRONT OF ME!~~

~~YOU~~ IN SPITE OF ~~ALL~~

COME BACK FOR EVEN MORE OF THE SAME?

YOU MUST BE PRECISELY

~~REQUIRE A MASOCHIST~~

MASOCHIST

YOU TO ~~LOVE~~ A MODERN LEPER

ON HIS LAST LEG ~~~~ PERHAPS YOU

ON HIS LAST LEG ALWAYS WILL

"THE MODERN LEPER"

A cripple walks amongst you all, you tired human beings
he's got all the things a cripple has not, two working
arms and legs.
Vital parts fall from his system and dissolve in
Scottish rain
vitally he doesn't miss them he's too fucked up to care.

Is that you in front of me
coming back for even more of exactly the same?
You must be a masochist to love a modern leper on his
last leg.

I crippled your heart a hundred times and still can't
work out why
you see, I've got this disease that I can't shake and
I'm just rattling through life.
This is how we do things now, this is how the modern
stay scared
so I cut out all the good stuff, I cut off my foot to
spite my leg.

Is that you in front of me
coming back for even more of exactly the same?
you must be a masochist to love a modern leper on his
last leg.
I am ill but I'm not dead
I don't know which of those I prefer
because that limb which I have lost
it was the only thing holding me up, holding me up.

I'm lying on the ground now
and you walk in through the only door
I have lost my eyesight like I said I would,
but I still know.

That that is you in front of me
and you are back for even more of exactly the same
are you a masochist?
You love a modern leper on his last leg.
You're not ill and I'm not dead
doesn't that make us the perfect pair?
You should sit with me, and we'll start again
and you can tell me all about what you did today,
what you did today.

"I FEEL BETTER"

I left Howse without a fucking clue
and left New York City, girl, without you
but the sun does shine in this place some days
and even when there's cloud there isn't always rain.

I'll stow away my greys
in a padlocked case, in a padlocked room
only to be released
when I sing all the songs I wrote about you
this is the last one that I'll do.

Now I'm free in parentheses
I'm not sure what I ought to do with it
it sits in the house, bright eyes and raised hand
if I ignore its advances then the hand goes down.

I'll stow away my greys
in a padlocked case and in a padlocked room
only to be released
when I sing all the songs I wrote about you
this is the last that one I'll do.

I feel better and better and worse and then better
than ever, than ever, than ever
I feel much better, and better, and worse and then better
than ever, than ever, than ever, than ever...

I'll stow away my greys
in a padlocked case and in a padlocked room
only to be released
when I see you walking 'round with someone new
this is the last song, this is the last song
this is the last song I'll write about you.

618-2013156/02

I FLED HOUSE WITHOUT A FUCKING CLUE
BUT I LEFT NEW YORK CITY, GIRL, WITHOUT YOU
~~I'M JUST SAD BECAUSE I FEEL~~ ~~BUT~~ QUITE GOOD ~~BUT~~ THE SUN DOES MAKE
~~AND ITS~~ ~~SO~~ SAD TO ~~KNOW THAT YOU DO~~ TOO SOUND IN THIS ~~FEEL~~
~~I'T~~ ~~SOMEWHAT~~ ~~SAD THAT~~ ~~WE FEEL~~ ~~THIS GOOD~~. SOUND ~~AND DOES~~
~~THIS KILL THE PEOPLE~~. AND ~~EVERY~~ ~~WHEN THERE'S~~
CLOUD THERE ISN'T ALWAYS
RAIN.
~~I'VE FOUND~~ ~~THAT~~ ~~SILVER LINING FRAME IS TRUE~~.
~~STOW THEM~~ ~~THESE~~ ~~GREYS~~ STOW AWAY MY GREYS
~~GIVE IT FREELY~~ ~~MISERABLE FOR~~ ~~KEPT~~ IN A PADLOCKED CASE IN A PADLOCKED ROOM
~~I'M~~ ~~GIVING UP THE GREYS~~ ~~STOW AWAY MY GREYS~~ ONLY TO BE
~~OR JUST OPEN SOME TO~~ ~~LET THE SUN RAIN~~ RELEASED

WHEN I SING ~~THE~~ SONGS I WROTE ABOUT YOU
~~IN~~ THIS I THE LAST ONE THAT I'LL DO

NOW THAT I'M "FREE" IN PARENTHESIS
I'M NOT SURE ~~WHAT~~ I ~~EVEN~~ TO DO WITH IT BRIGHT EYES + RAISED HAND
IT SITS IN THE ~~HOUSE~~ ~~PUTS UP ITS HAND~~ ~~WHEREVER~~
~~FOR NOW~~ ~~I'LL IGNORE ITS~~ ~~ADVANCES~~ ~~IT PUTS IT BACK DOWN~~
IF I ~~JUST~~ IGNORE ITS ADVANCES THEN THE HAND GOES DOWN.

~~I SCRATCH MY HEAD AND WONDER WHAT FREE MEANS~~

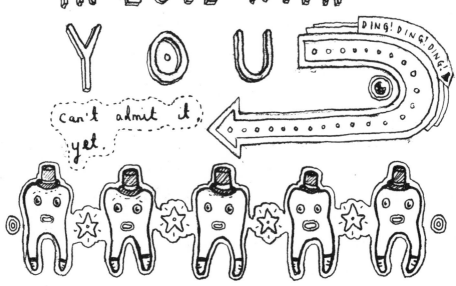

"GOOD ARMS vs. BAD ARMS"

Good arms versus bad arms, I win hands down, down
they are built to hold and fit,
look how far they go around.
You don't need these now that you've found another pair
and the difference is astounding I should expect, except ...

Leave the rest at arm's length
keep your naked flesh under your favourite dress
leave the rest at arm's length
when they reach out, don't touch them, don't touch them.

I decided this decision some six months ago
so I'll stick to my guns but from now on it's war.
I am armed with the past and the will and a brick
I might not want you back, but I want to kill him.

Leave the rest at arm's length
keep your naked flesh under your favourite dress
leave the rest at arm's length
when they reach out, don't touch them, don't touch them.

Leave the rest at arm's length
don't brush with him, he might have diseases
leave the rest at arm's length
steer clear of the grasp, girl
run, run away.

Leave the rest at arm's length
just roll over boy, don't make me do this
leave the rest at arm's length
I am armed to the teeth, I am heavy-set.

Leave the rest at arm's length
I'm not ready to see you this happy
leave the rest at arm's length
I am still in love with you, can't admit it yet.

"FAST BLOOD"

Good night, it's stroke time
let's get paralysed down both sides.
Snake hips, red city kiss
your black eyes roll back.
Midnight organ fight
yours gives in to mine
it's all right.

The fast blood
hurricanes through me
and then rips my roof away with a fire hiss
this is the longest kiss goodnight.

And now I tremble
because this fumble has become biblical.
I feel like I just died twice
and was reborn again for our dirty sins.

The fast blood, fast blood, fast blood
hurricanes through me
and then rips my roof away with a fire hiss
this is the longest kiss goodnight, goodnight.

I fall down, back and forth to the end
And I hold on, it's all gone and she said to me,
She said good night"

FAST BLOOD

GOOD NIGHT
ITS STROKE TIME
~~FEATHER LIGHT~~ ~~~~
~~GET~~ ~~PARALYSED DOWN~~ ~~BORN~~ ~~BOTH~~ SIDES
~~LOVING~~ BLACK EYES
~~~~ ROLL BACK
SNAKE HIPS
RED ~~~~ CITY KISS

~~~~
~~~~ ~~HOT FRESH~~ ~~~~ MIDNIGHT
~~~~ ~~OUT~~ ~~RED~~ ORGAN FIGHT
~~KEEP~~ ~~~~ YOURS PLAYS NEXT TO MINE.
~~BREATHE~~ SO NICE.
~~BREAK IN AGAIN~~

~~FAST BLOOD~~ ~~~~ SHIT HOT BODY
~~TEARS~~ ~~~~ ~~~~ VEINS
HURRICANES THROUGH ~~~~ IT RIPS OUR ROOF ~~AWAY~~ ~~PLAY~~
~~~~ ~~~~ WIDE ~~~~
~~INTO A FIRE KISS~~ THIS IS THAT LONG KISS
GOODNIGHT.

~~SO~~ ~~KISS~~ NOW
I TREMBLE
THIS FUMBLE
BECAME BIBLICAL

I FEEL LIKE
I DIED THEN
FAR ~~MY~~ SINS
AND WAS REBORN AGAIN.

~~BLOOD~~ ~~SLOW DOWN~~ IN A SHIT HOT BODY.
~~FASTER~~ ~~~~ ~~ORGAN~~
~~FASTER~~ ~~TOO~~ ~~ROUND THE BRAIN~~
~~SLOW~~ BLOOD T~~~~ ~~~~.
~~SLOW~~ ~~BLOOD~~ UP HURRICANES THROUGH VEINS
~~~~ RIPS THE ROOF AWAY
INTO A FIRE ~~KISS~~
THIS IS THAT ~~LONG~~ KISS
GOODNIGHT

THE
GIVE ME SOFT SOFT STATIC OF THE OPEN FIRE + THE SHUFFLE OF OUR FEET
+ ~~TAKE CARE~~ OF ~~YOUR LAUGHTER IN ANY~~ ?
~~...~~ AND GET OLD OLD OLD FASHIONED.
DO IT LIKE THEY DID IN 43

"OLD OLD FASHIONED"

Turn off the TV
it's killing us, we never speak
there's a radio in the corner
it's dying to make us see.

So give me soft, soft static
with a human voice underneath
and we can both get old fashioned
put the brakes on these fast, fast wheels.

Let's get old fashioned
back to how things used to be
if I get old, old fashioned
would you get old, old fashioned with me?

Put the wall clock in the top drawer
turn off the lights so we can see
we will waltz across the carpet
1-2-3-2-2-3.

So give me the soft, soft static
of the open fire and the shuffle of our feet
we can both get old fashioned
do it like they did in '43.

Let's get old fashioned
back to how things used to be
if I get old, old fashioned
would you get old, old fashioned with me?

So give me soft, soft static
we won't need no electricity
if we both get old fashioned
we won't have to rely on our memories.

Oh let's get old fashioned
back to how things used to be
if I get old, old fashioned
would you get old, old fashioned with me?

"THE TWIST"

Do the twist in the twisting outfit
the loose tie with the loose limp wrists
lift your dress enough to show me those shins
let your hair stick to your forehead.

Did you blush then when our hips touched?
I can't tell, we are already red
am I right, are you giving me the signs?
Is that pink mist or just lit dry ice?

Twist and whisper the wrong name
I don't care and nor do my ears.
Twist yourself around me
I need company, I need human heat
I need human heat.

Let's pretend I'm attractive and then
you won't mind, we can twist for a while
it's the night I can be who you like
and I'll quietly leave before it gets light.

So twist and whisper the wrong name
I don't care and nor do my ears.
Twist yourself around me
I need company, I need human heat
I need human heat ...

It's the mmm hmm aha, extrasupervery

Twist and whisper the right name
I'm Dave, if you please
the twist is that you're just like me
you need company, you need human heat
you need human heat.

GOD'S
GOT HIS DEAD FRIENDS

GOD'S
GOT HIS DEAD FRIENDS
ROUND

"HEAD ROLLS OFF"

Jesus is just a Spanish boy's name
how come one man got so much fame?
To any me, it's pointless to anybody
that doesn't have faith
give me the cloth and I'll wipe my face.

When it's all gone
something carries on
and it's not morbid at all
just when nature's had enough of you.

When my blood stops
someone else's will have not
when my head rolls off
someone else's will turn
and while I'm alive,
I'll make tiny changes to earth.

So you can burn me
'cause we'll all be the same, the same way
dirt in someone's eye that's cried down the drain
I believe in a house in the clouds
and God's got his dead friends 'round
he's painted all the walls in red
to remind them they're all dead.

And you know when it's all gone
something carries on
and it's not morbid at all
just when nature's had enough of you.

When my blood stops
someone else's will have not
when my head rolls off
someone else's will turn
you can mark my words,
I'll make changes to earth.

While I'm alive,
I'll make tiny changes to earth ...

618-2013156/08

"MY BACKWARDS WALK"

I'm working on my backwards walk
walking with no shoes or socks
and as the time rewinds to the end of May
I wish we'd never met then met today.

I'm working on my faults and cracks
filling in the blanks and gaps
when I write them out they don't make sense
I need you to pencil in the rest.

I'm working on drawing a straight line
and I'll draw until I get one right
it's bold and dark, girl, can't you see?
I've done drawn a line between you and me.

I'm working on erasing you
I just don't have the proper tools
I'll get hammered, forget that you exist
but there's no way I'm forgetting this.

I'm working hard on walking out
but my shoes keep sticking to the ground
my clothes won't let me close the door
'cause my trousers seem to love your floor.

I've been working on my backwards walk
'cause there's nowhere else for me to go
except back to you just one last time
say yes before I change my mind.

Say yes before I...

You're the shit and I'm knee-deep in it...

"KEEP YOURSELF WARM"

My hole, I'll get my hole
I'll get my hole
get my hole, get my hole
and I'll find out more.
It's a choo-choo train
a rocket launch
if we have a hormone race
I'm bound to finish first.

Can you see in the dark?
Can you see the look on your face?
The flashing white light's been turned off
you don't know who is in your bed.
It takes more than fucking someone you don't know
to keep warm
do you really think now for a house beat
you'll find your love in a hole?

You won't find love in a, won't find love in a hole
it takes more than fucking someone to keep yourself warm.

I'm drunk, I'm drunk
and you're probably on pills
if we both got the same diseases
it's irrelevant, girl.
The woo-hoo whistle steam
evaporates, disappears
my point of entry
is the same way that I leave.

Can you see in the dark?
Can you see the look on your face?
The flashing white light's been turned off
you don't know who is in your bed.
It takes more than fucking someone you don't know
to keep warm
do you really think now for a house beat
you'll find your love in a hole?

You won't find love in a, won't find love in a hole
it takes more than fucking someone to keep yourself warm.

You won't find love in a, won't find love in a hole
it takes more than fucking someone to keep yourself...

See in the dark
can you see the look on your face?
The flashing white light's been turned off
you don't know who is in your bed.
It takes more than fucking someone you don't know
to keep warm
do you really think now for a house beat
you'll find your love in a hole?

POKE AT MY EYELIDS.
WHY CAN'T I CRY ABOUT THIS?
MAYBE THERE'S SOMETHING THAT YOU KNOW THAT I DON'T

WE ADOPT A BRAND NEW LANGUAGE
~~COMMUNICATE~~
~~SPEAKING~~ THROUGH ~~THE~~ PURSED LIPS
~~AS~~ YOU TRY NOT TO PUT ON
ANY SEXY CLOTHES OR GLANCES
I'LL ~~EAT~~ NEVER CATCH A MOUSE ~~AND~~ TO
PRESENT ~~IT~~ ~~WITH IN MY~~ ~~IT~~ IN MY MOUTH AND
~~ANOTHER'S~~
MAKE YOU FEEL YOU DO
WITH SOMEONE AND BE ~~CLOSE~~ TO
BUT THERE'S ONE THING IF WE'VE GOT GOING ~~RE-ARRANGE~~
AND ITS THE ONLY THING THAT U KNOWING
ITS GOT LOTS TO DO WITH MAGNETS
~~BUT...~~ AND THE PULL OF THE MOON

WE CAN CHANGE OUR PARTNERS
~~IT~~ IS A PROGRESSING DANCE ~~BUT!~~

~~~~
~~~~
~~BUT~~ REMEMBER IT WAS
ME WHO DRESSED UP TO
THE SWEATY FLOUR.
OURS WAS BEEN A REEL ~~B~~ ~~REEL~~
~~~~
I'VE GOT
SHINSPLINTS AND A STITCH
FROM WE
BUT LIKE A DRUNKEN NIGHT
ITS THE BEST BITS THAT
ARE COLOURED IN.

~~~~
WHY ~~DON'T~~ LOUD ~~REEL~~ OVER
~~AND~~ OR CHOKE ON A BONE
~~AND~~ WE CAN MOURN ITS PASSING
~~~~
IN A WAKE WITH SNAKE
AND A BURY IT IN SNOW?

SHOULD WE TRY AND KICK ITS CUNT IN?
~~WIPE IT~~ DIE FROM ~~IT~~ ~~DISEASE~~
IF YOU DONT WANT TO BEWITH
I JUST SAY AND I WILL GO.

"POKE"

Poke at my iris, why can't I cry about this?
Maybe there is something that you know that I don't
we adopt brand new language,
communicate through pursed lips
and you try not to put on any sexy clothes or graces.
I might never catch a mouse and present it in my mouth
to make you feel you're with someone who deserves to be
with you
but there's one thing we've got going and it's the only
thing worth knowing
it's got lots to do with magnets and the pull of the moon.
Why won't our love keel over as it chokes on a bone?
And we can mourn its passing and then bury it in snow
or should we kick its cunt in and watch as it dies
from bleeding?
If you don't want to be with me just say and I will go.

We can change our partners, this is a progressive dance but
remember it was me who dragged you up to the sweaty floor
this has been a reel, I've got shin-splints and a stitch
from we
but like a drunken night it's the best bits that are
coloured in.
You should look through some old photos, I adored you in
every one of those
if someone took a picture of us now they'd need to be told
that we had ever clung and tied a navy knot with arms
at night
I'd say she was his sister but she doesn't have his nose
and now we're unrelated and rid of all the shit we hated
but I hate when I feel like this and I never hated you.

"FLOATING IN THE FORTH"

So you just stepped out of the front of my house
and I'll never see you again
I closed my eyes for a second and when they opened
you weren't there.
And the door shut shut I was vacuum-packed
shrink-wrapped out of air
and the spine collapsed and the eyes rolled back
to stare at my starving brain.

Fully clothed, I'll float away
down the Forth, into the sea
I think I'll save suicide for another day.

I picture this corpse on the M8 hearse
and I have found a way to sleep
on a rolled-up coat against the window
with the strobe of the sun and the life I've led.
Am I ready to leap? Is there peace beneath
the roar of the Forth Road Bridge?
On the northern side is a Fife of mine
and a boat in the port for me.

Fully clothed, I'll float away
down the Forth, into the sea
I'll steer myself through chopping waves
as manic gulls scream, 'It's okay!'
Take your life, give it a shake
and gather up all your loose change.

I think I'll save suicide for another year.

"WHO'D YOU KILL NOW?"

Who'd you push down the stairs last night?
I would've liked to have been a part of that

Who'd you push down the stairs last night?
I would've liked to have been a part of that

AROOOOOO OOO OOOOO !

& !

IT'S...

...THE 'AND' TIT

SHIT HAWK

THE SHIT·HAWK
(ASS MOUNTED)

"DON'T"

Please don't leave me, don't forget me my girl
don't leave me here.
Please don't leave me, don't desert me my girl
don't leave me here.
Don't leave me, don't smoke cigarettes and don't taunt
the geese
I don't need me, don't forget me my girl,
don't leave me here
in my front room
in my front room
in my heart, heart.

Please don't leave me, don't forget me my girl
don't leave me here.
Please don't leave me, don't desert me my girl
don't leave me here.
Don't believe me when I say I don't care,
'cause I do need this
don't leave me, don't forget me my girl,
don't leave me here
in my front room
in my front room
in my heart, oh ...

In my front room
in my front room
in my front room
in my front room
in my front room.

                    618-2013156/B/15

"SOON GO"

There's someone on top of you fucking
chuck me or I'm stuck here.
Every sixth month it seems
my mind goes over my turgidity

I'll soon go
I'll be lost in the thoughts of tomorrow
and my warm heart, it will soon grow cold
and I won't be old
I'll soon go

You admit, you admit
it's worse this way, it's worse with me.
Work with my shit
would you rather work elsewhere?

I'll soon go
I'll be lost in the thoughts of tomorrow
your warm heart will have long grown cold
you won't be old
you'll soon go

I check for a death beneath my bed at night
I'm not scared of dying
I'm afraid I've lost my life

Soon go
we're still lost in the thoughts of tomorrow
and our warm hearts will have soon grown cold
so let's make the most
we'll soon go.

TOP :SOON GO: LINES... EVER! EVER! EVER!

#1 I'LL TAKE BACK WHAT I SHOPLIFTED [BUT THEN]
   I WON'T TAKE BACK A THING I'VE SAID.

FAKE FAKE BUS + SIRENS,

#2 THERE IS A JOB I'LL TAKE IT
   I VOLUNTEER MY SERVICES AND GIVE YOU MY LIKE.

#3 BUT MY SECONDS THOUGHTS DON'T OFTEN WORK
   WAIT AROUND NOW FOR MY THIRD OR FOURTH.

#4 THIS IS TOO LATE WORK US DECIDES
   DO US WANDER OFF OR SPRINT BY LIFE'S SIDE.

#5 HERE COMES THE BACK BIG OF OUR LIFE
   I'LL TAKE LEFT, THINK WILL YOU CHOOSE RIGHT?

#6 WILL YOU BE WITH ME NOVEMBER 17TH.
   I'VE HEARD THE WORLD MAY END THAT DAY

#7 AT MY WORLD'S END THERE WON'T BE A WARNING BEEP.
   I HOPE MY LAST WORDS AND ACTIONS ARE BETTER THAN THESE

#8 AS THE SIREN SOUNDS AND THE WORLD ENDS
   RUSH FOR YOUR LOVED ONE, EVAPORATE WITH SOMEONE ELSE.

#9 I'VE WASTED TOO MUCH OF YOUR TIME ON THIS
   DO I WASTE MONTHS MORE AND SUFFER YEARS OF REGRETS?

#10 I SIRENS AT THE WORLD'S CLOSE (THE)
    + I IMAGING YOUR FACE IN MY HANDS LIT (BY) BRIGHT (BY) WORLD COURT.

#11 WE ARE ON A HILL AT THE END OF HOLOCAUST.
    JUST EXPIRE WITH ME AS THE WARHEAD GOES OFF.

#12 EVERY NIGHT IS THE EVE OF OUR LAST.
    IF I COMPARE TWO DAYS, THE ONES WITH YOU ARE EASILY TYPED BEST.

#13 AND AS OUR EXPIRY CLOSES IN
    WE ALL CRAM THE LOST YEARS INTO THE DAYS BEFORE DEATH

#14 I THINK I'LL STOP HAVING SLEEP INS
    EACH SUNDOWN BRINGS THE EVE OF APOCALYPSE.

#15 I MIGHT CHANGE MY MIND FROM VERSE TO VERSE WE SEE COULD BE THE
    BUT LET THE LAST POST AND WORMS EXPLAIN MYSELF BEST.

#16: EACH BLINK COULD BRING THE CURTAIN DOWN ON LIFE
SO LIVE LIKE YOU'RE STARING AT THE HOLE IN A
GUN; AND DON'T CLOSE YOUR EYES

#17: I'VE NEVER QUITE HAD TO IMAGINE ~~WHATEVER ELSE~~ HOW BAD WOULD
~~IT~~ ~~TASTE LIKE~~ TASTE
IF YOU ~~FUCKED OFF~~ ~~FUCKED~~ LET GO MY HAND AND
I NEVER SAW YOUR FACE AGAIN,

#18: INSIDE THE BUNKER AS THE WORLD ENDS ABOVE
— WE MIGHT GO GOING WITH IT, LET'S BE ONE PILE OF DUST.

O
#19: THERE ARE TIMES I FEEL MY HEART ~~MIGHT~~ START TO ATTACK
BEFORE ~~IT~~ KILLS ME, ~~WHEN IT JUST COME BACK!~~
WE WILL HAVE TO MOB FAST.

#20: IN EACH DUSK, ARE ~~THE~~ USED THREATS OF THE ~~LIFE END~~ END
PACK YOUR SUITCASE, WE'RE NOT SLEEPING OF LIFE TONITE.

#21 BUT THERE'S MY BRAIN I THINK OF A LOT THAT
WHAT DAMN PLACE ON ~~THE~~ HEAD, REGRET 'DIDS' NOT
YOUNG 'DID NOTS'

#22 I'LL LOOK FORWARD TO 0 BOTH
AS THE FIRST TIME I CAN ASSESS THIS MESS.

#23 THERE MAY A TIMEBOMB IN MY HEAD
BUT I DON'T THINK THAT'S ~~LIKE~~ I ~~HEAR A CONTANT~~ HEAR A CONTANT
WHOD TICK.

#24 I HEAR TICKS A AWAKE IN BED.
AS I LIE
IS IT THE WALLCLOCK OR IS THERE 0 BOMB IN HERE?

#25 I AM PLAGUED BY ~~THE COGS~~ TO THE COGS A ~~DEA~~ A CONSTANT TICK
ITS THE SOUND OF THE COUNTDOWN TO A QUIET DEATH

#26 I CHECK BENEATH MY BED FOR ~~THE BOMB~~ BOMBS EVERY NIGHT
~~THEN NO~~'S I'M ONLY SCARED OF DYING AND
NOT SAYING THIS

#27 AND I LIVE FOR VALUES SURROUNDING MY EARS
YOU'VE GOT TO DESTROY IT ALL BEFORE YOU REBUILD

#28: I KNOW AS A PROMISE, THIS ~~WON'T PROMISE~~ MY
DOESN'T SOUND
I ~~WONT~~ BUT IF YOU WANT ME PROMISING

REF	618-202315134.
ARTIST	FRIGHTENED RABBIT
TITLE	"The Winter Of Mixed Drinks"

MONTH / YEAR

MAR 1 0 2010

"THINGS"

Here is the evidence of human existence
a splitting bin bag next to two damp boxes
and I cannot find a name for them
they hardly show that I have lived
and the dust it settles on these things,
displays my age again
like a new skin made from old skin that had barely been
lived in

I didn't need these things, I didn't need them
pointless artefacts from a mediocre past
so I shed my clothes, I shed my flesh down to the bone
and burned the rest
I didn't need these things, I didn't need them
took them all to bits, turned them outside in
and I left them on the floor and ran for dear life
through the door

The useless objects, they gathered a storm of shit
a dim and silent shed full of your life's supplies
when all you need's a coffin and your Sunday best to
smarten up the end
at the front gate, what a reward awaits?
One bite of loaf from a holy ghost
an eternity of suffering the company of all those
Christian men

I didn't need these things, I didn't need them
pointless artefacts from a mediocre past
so I shed my clothes, I shed my flesh down to the bone
and burned the rest
I didn't need these things, I didn't need them
took them all to bits, turned them outside in
and I left them on the floor and ran for dear life
through the door

I'll never need these things, I'll never need them
it's just you I need
you, my human heat
and the things are only things and nothing brings me
like you bring me
I'll never need these things, I'll never need them
never going back
so we can drop the past
and we'll leave it on the floor and run for dear life
through the door.

"SWIM UNTIL YOU CAN'T SEE LAND"

A salute at the threshold of the North Sea, of my mind
and a nod to the boredom that drove me here to face the
tide and swim ...

Dip a toe in the ocean, oh how it hardens, and it numbs
the rest of me is a version of man built to collapse and
crumb
if I hadn't come now to the coast to disappear
I may have died in the landslide of rocks and hopes and
fears

So, swim until you can't see land
swim until you can't see land
swim until you can't see land
are you a man, are you a bag of sand?

Up to my knees now, do I wade? Do I dive?
The sea has seen my like before though, it's my first
and perhaps last time
let's call me a Baptist, call this a drowning of the
past
she is there on the shoreline throwing stones at my back

So, swim until you can't see land
swim until you can't see land
swim until you can't see land
are you a man, are you a bag of sand?

Now the water is taller than me and the land is a marker
line
all I am, is a body adrift in water, salt and sky

So, swim until you can't see land
swim until you can't see land
swim until you can't see land
are you a man, are you a bag of sand?

"THE LONELINESS AND THE SCREAM"

Can you hear the road from this place?
Can you hear footsteps, voices?
Can you see the blood on my sleeve?
I have fallen in the forest, did you hear me?

In the loneliness
oh, the loneliness
and the scream to prove to everyone that I exist
in the loneliness
oh, the loneliness
and the scream to bring the blood to the front of my
face again

Am I here? Of course I am, yes
all I need is your hand to drag me out again
it wasn't me, I didn't dig this ditch
I was walking for weeks before I fell in

to the loneliness
oh, the loneliness
and the scream to prove to everyone that I exist
in the loneliness
oh, the loneliness
and the scream to fill a thousand black balloons
with air

We fall down, find God just to lose it again
glue the community together, we were hammering it
I fell down, found love, I can lose it again
but now our communal heart beats miles from here.

THE WRESTLE

THIS CRUMPLED OCEAN IS ÷ NO BOAT TRIP
DARK~~ENOUGH~~ WATER STOLE – MY CLOTHING
A SHAPE STIRS – BENEATH ME
~~A~~ PULSE POUNDS – ~~AND~~ ALONG BLOOD STREAMS
THE FIRST BITE MARKS ~~A~~ THE BEGINNING OF
THE CLOTHELESS WRESTLE WITH THE CLOTHELESS ANIMAL.
~~LET BONE TIGHTEEN TO ME~~ PLEASE ~~MAY ENTER~~
~~IN IF YOU CAN EXPLAIN OF IT CAN EXPLAIN FEAR~~ (?)
~~AND~~ THIS IS THE TEST I – LEFT HAND FOR
TO GRIP FLESH AND – PULL MUSCLE. (IN).
(IN) THE VICE CLINCH ~~NO EVER~~ ~~WON'T~~ OF THE STRUGGLE
I WON'T GIVE IN ~~SUBMIT~~ TO THE WEIGHT ~~STRENGTH~~ OF
~~&~~ THE CLOTHELESS WRESTLE WITH THE CLOTHELESS ANIMAL

MY ENEMY – PLEASE STAY CLOSE TO ME
I'VE NO BREATH LEFT – YOU COULD BREATH THIEF
THE LAST ~~LAST~~ GASPS FROM – A BURST LUNG.
THE FIGHT FATHERS – A WEAK SON
~~AND A LAST FLAVOUR OF SALT THE~~ THE LAST TASTE OF SALT ~~FALLS OF THE~~ IN MY MOUTH.
SKIN BREAKS – WITH NO SOUND.
I AM TORN LIMB FROM LIMB
THERE IS BONE – THERE'S GRISTLE AND SPIT.
IN THE CLOTHELESS WRESTLE WITH THE CLOTHELESS
ANIMAL.

"THE WRESTLE"

The crumpled ocean is no boat trip
the dark water stole my clothing

A shape stirs beneath me
a pulse pounds along bloodstreams
the first bite marks the beginning of
the clotheless wrestle with the clotheless animal

Bare those teeth to me please, maneater
you can see all of me, naked with fear

This is the test I left land for
to grip flesh and pull muscle in
the vice clinch of the struggle
I can't give in to the weight of
the clotheless wrestle with the clotheless animal

My enemy, please stay close to me
I've no breath left, you cold breath thief

The last gasp from a burst lung
the fight fathers a weak son
the last taste of salt in my mouth
skin breaks, with no sound

I am torn limb from limb
there is bone, there is gristle, and spit
in the clotheless wrestle with the clotheless animal.

"SKIP THE YOUTH"

I've been digging that hole tonight
on my knees beneath the moon
all I need is a place to lie
guess a grave will have to do.
Won't you give me two minutes please?
Just let me cover my eyes
all the hammer and scrape has been chipping away
at the lustre of life

(Move! Move!)
I would but I am so tired
(Move! Move!)
If I can't shake myself, I can't dance with you

Though my body is far from old
I'm bound to useless youth
and I can't fake a fist to throw
through the crust of the Earth.
If you find me, don't wake me
I can't be shaken awake
if you don't stare at the dark, if you never feel bleak
life starts to lose its taste

(Move! Move!)
I would but I am so tired
(Move! Move!)
If I can't shake myself, I can't dance with you

(I hear drums!)
The worn-out beat of a tired heart
(You are young!)
If this is the prime of life, I wish I could skip the
blasted youth

Skip the youth, it's ageing me too much ...

 618-202315134/05

MOVE! MOVE! (SKIP THE YOUTH).

I'VE BEEN DIGGING THAT HOLE TONIGHT
ON MY KNEES BENEATH THE MOON
ALL I NEED IS A PLACE TO LIE
GUESS A GRAVE WILL HAVE TO DO.
_____

AND I DON'T WANT TO BE FOUND SO I.
MAKE A BED BENEATH? THE DIRT.
                  UNDER?
UNDERSTAND I DON'T WANT TO DIE
JUST DON'T WANT TO BE DISTURBED.

MOVE! MOVE! I KNOW I HAVE MY BREATH I, KNOW I SHOULD LOOK ALIVE
MOVE! MOVE! — I JUST DO NOT LOVE MYSELF, I DO NOT LOVE LIFE.
                                          TODAY

I AM NEITHER THOUGH THIS BODY IS FAR FROM OLD
I AM BOUND IN USELESS YOUTH
WHERE YOU CAN'T MAKE A FIST TO THROW
          I
THROUGH THE CRUST OF THE EARTH
_____

AND IF YOU FIND ME DON'T SHAKE ME (I)
I CAN'T BE SHAKEN AWAKE
IF YOU DON'T TASTE THE DARK
IF YOU NEVER FEEL BLEAK
LIFE STARTS TO LOSE ITS TASTE.

YOU ARE YOUNG STILLBORN YOUTH IN MY DUMB ... IS LEFT IN MY
YOUTH IS LOST IN MY ...
... TOO ... BEAT OF A ... HEART
I NEED ... — I HEAR DRUMS THE LORD ... A TIRED HEART.
MOVE! MOVE! — I CANNOT LIFT MY DEAD I CANNOT LIFT THIS WORK ...
GO! GO! — IF THIS IS THE PRIME OF LIFE I WISH I COULD SKIP THE YOUTH
               IT'S AGING ME TOO MUCH.

"NOTHING LIKE YOU"

This is a story, and you are not in it, uh-huh
flock of pages torn out.
Here is a bedroom that you've never been in and
here's your shovel, there's the ground.
Look, two lovers covered in covers, uh-huh
I can put us to bed tonight
I am bruised but she is dressing my wounds
night nursing a broken man

She was not the cure for cancer
and all of my questions still ask for answers
but there is nothing like someone new
and this girl, she was nothing like you

After waking up post-operation I found
I had come in a dream again
all the pain almost as painful as ever but
something in me was not the same.
At night during dreams of submission I could
claw back my heart and soul
as the size of the tumour diminishes
so we fill that black hole

She was not the cure for cancer
and all of my questions still ask for answers
but there is nothing like someone new
and this girl, she was nothing like you.

618-202315134/06

"FOOTSHOOTER"

The booze in my blood runs fast and loud
and my brain shouts down to my mouth
'Say whatever I think. Say it at him.'
When the dam bursts open and you're drowned out, boy
better go outside, sit in your boat and wait
'til you get washed away

Hold onto your thumbs
tighten your eyelids
lock up your ears, my dear, I'm verbal when I am loaded
duck under that desk
cover your neck
thicken your skin as I begin to shoot myself in the
foot again

And as the body succumbs and my mouth goes numb
I limp out to the sound of the breaking of broken toes
a vandal spoke.
And in the stark and the sobering dry sunlight
I will blink my eyes and hope the blink can erase
all the shit that I said and did

Hold onto your thumbs
tighten your eyelids
lock up your ears, my dear, I'm verbal when I am loaded
duck under that desk
cover your neck
thicken your skin as I begin to shoot myself in the
foot again

If I shoot at you, you should shoot at me, too
and we can drown in pools of the thick dark words we
threw
and as my face turns white, I apologise
I am sorry
it's not your fault
it's mine

Hold onto your thumbs
tighten your eyelids
lock up your ears, my dear, I'm verbal when I am loaded
duck under that desk
cover your neck
thicken your skin as I begin to shoot myself in the
foot again.

"NOT MISERABLE"

This is easier now
I have found all the pieces that I lost in the flood
it wasn't that much.
And though it's easier now
I will always remember the night that I almost drowned
all alone in a house

And the love that I lost
with all of the shit that came out in the wash
just a pocket of fluff.
I am not put upon
I am free from disease no greys, no liver-spots
most of the misery's gone
gone, gone to the bone

I'm not miserable now
and no one knows
no one knows
I'm not miserable

So the hymns that I've sung
prayers for the fucked from a bitter forked tongue
sing of history now.
Though the corners are lit
the dark can return with the flick of a switch
it hasn't turned on me yet

I'm not miserable now
and no one knows
no one knows
I'm not miserable.

LIVING IN (NGIR) HORNS! SOMBY!
COLOUR

live - living in colour... Don't

I can see the paint on your toes   FUCKING
ever ~~in~~ the blackout I know.   FORGET

(as)
(I am floating I - I) am floating with my eyes closed
with its sails
(And I am soaking I - I) am weathered by the winter
of mixed drinks
(Am I dancing am - am) or am I simply spinning
in my own grave.
(You are ~~asking you~~) you are ~~asking~~ and with 2 steps
I'm ~~saved~~

(Weeks gone by I was weak) & I was paler
than a pine box that holds bones
She poked the iris then   come rushing
pierced ~~poked~~ a hole & watched the colour ~~pour~~ forth.

(Modern moderna mod - modern)
~~held~~ my head in warm hands
with pink nails
Mopped the mouth - mop mop!
whispered that the sickness will go away.

BLEB: a bubble in glass.

"LIVING IN COLOUR"

Living in colour, live living in colour
I can see the paint on your toes
Living in colour, live living in colour
even in the blackout, I know

I am floating
with my eyes closed, with no sails
I am soaking
I am weathered by the winter of mixed drinks.
Am I dancing?
Or am I simply spinning in my own grave?
You are asking
and with two steps, I'm saved

Living in colour, live living in colour
I can see the paint on your toes
Living in colour, live living in colour
even in the blackout, I know

Weeks gone by, I was weak
I was paler than a pine box that holds bones
she poked the iris
then she pierced a hole and watched the colour
rush forth.
Modern Madonna
held my head in warm hands with pink nails
mopped my mouth
and whispered that the sickness will go away

Living in colour, live living in colour
I can see the paint on your toes
Living in colour, live living in colour
even in the blackout, I know
Living in colour, live living in colour
I can see the paint on your toes
Living in colour, live living in colour
even as I black out, I know

And though I dreamt with a rapid eye
by day I hoped to rapidly die
and have my organs laid on ice

wait for somebody that would treat them right
but as the night started swallowing
you pulled the blood to my blue lip
forced the life through still veins
filled my heart with red again

Living in colour, live living in colour
I can see the paint on your toes
Living in colour, live living in colour
even in the blackout, I know
Living in colour, live living in colour
I can see the paint on your toes
Living in colour, live living in colour
even as I black out, I know.

FILLED my HEART WITH RED
AGAIN.

TABLE DES MATIÈRES

"YES, I WOULD"

My cry for a fistful of sand
breeds silence
hold me, I'm folding, I can't see land
the world just blinks
lead me, I'm stupid from a lesson learned
you've learned nothing
you told me to get lost to find myself

First it bleeds then it scabs
I feel like a haemophiliac
would I change if you carried me back?
Yes, I would
believe me now
yes, I would
I can't sink now
yes, I would

What if I am never thrown that rope?
And what if this tear in my side just pours and pours
and pours?
I wonder if they'd notice that I'm not around
the loss of a lonely man never makes much of a sound

First it bleeds then it scabs
I feel like a haemophiliac
would I change if you carried me back?
Yes, I would
believe me now
yes, I would
I can't sink now
yes, I would.

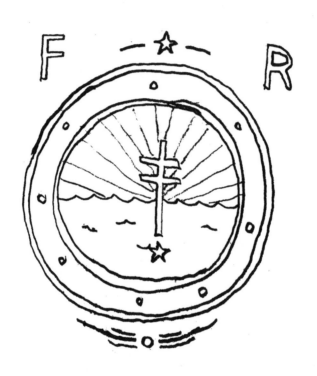

REF	618-202315134.
ARTIST	FRIGHTENED RABBIT
TITLE	"The Winter Of Mixed Drinks" B-Sides

MONTH / YEAR

NOV 1 6 2009

FEB 2 2 2010

"FUN STUFF"

I took off my clothes
she took off hers too
with no fanfares
and no hallelujahs
throughout the night
I would grind away the truth

But there's nothing sadder
than sad, sad sex
and the bad, bad news
is that I gave in
to the ugly hand
that first led me away from you

The fun stuff
is not so fun without you

So I drink until
I fill my brim
but there's nothing
fills me up the same
as a tiny word
broadcast across the sea

And should I go out
to dance tonight?
Well, my two left feet
need your two right
or I'll spin around
in circles endlessly

The fun stuff
is not so fun without you

Well, the city was born
bright blue today
and I whistled through
the sunlit streets

618-202315134/2194519

and my empty hand
felt cold and underused

And I'm quite all right
I get by just fine
I'm not depressed
not most of the time
it's just the fun stuff
is much less fun without you

The fun stuff
is much less fun without you.

"LEARNED YOUR NAME"

I wish I had, I wish I had
learned your name
but I couldn't read, I couldn't speak
ah, nobody taught me
met you when you were full of lemonade
you strode boldly in bold clothes
covered the fear
spent four years inside you
day upon day
you pushed colours and borders
lit by my gaze
oh, the photograph
the last gasp on steps at the end
just a tiny glance
all I ask
amidst all this tension
the old man visits every day
it's barely a love affair
he may love me
but I do not love him
can I move to where you move?
Dash down the stream
you threw the greed that I gave you
for all you gave me
you've demolished my heart
whichever room it lived in
oh, I wish I had, I wish I had
I wish I had learned your name.

618-202315134/2194519

REF	618-1618516.
ARTIST	FRIGHTENED RABBIT
TITLE	"A Frightened Rabbit EP"
MONTH / YEAR	OCT 31 2011

"SCOTTISH WINDS"

Come gather in my lungs, Scottish winds
belt out your blackest poems
as the sea around you sings
when that drone takes to the air
a single note to raise my hair
carry songs beyond my lungs
cold Scottish wind

Come fall upon my shoulders, Scottish rain
and dissolve all of the worry
that has hunched this back of mine
so let the hurt run down the drain to the reservoir
one day I'll add a drop of my own worries
to a dram

Gather heavy in these lungs, Scottish winds
all the fag smoke in the ether
of the grouse has clipped your wings
and I will cough just like my granddad
and his grandpa before him
ah, blow youth into these lungs
old Scottish winds

Come burl around my body, Scottish blood
I'll try not to spill a drop
oh, I'm sure you've spilled enough
and the English fucking rule
will mean nothing to these towns
ah, run forever in my veins
bold Scottish blood

And then whisper to my mouth, soft Scottish winds
just enough to say I love you
to the girl who keeps me sane
take the stupid things I've said
blow them miles and miles away
thank you in advance, Scottish winds
thank you in advance, Scottish winds.

IN THE PERFUMED ARMPIT
    OF THE TOWN
DEVELOPED BUT DEAD, NOW
THE PEOPLE ARE (THE) BRICKS
SIX FACED STONES, WRAPPED UP
~~WRAPPED~~ ~~UP LIKE~~ &
                    SAVED
SUCH DISAPPOINTMENT
WHEN THE PAPER IS RIPPED

AND SO I STAND, STILL BORING & BORED
I T CHUCK MY EYE ~~AND~~ DOWN, ~~AT THE~~
                    ~~AS WE CAN~~
                AGAINST A
                WALL

"FUCK THIS PLACE"

(with Tracyanne Campbell)

An itch, in my eye
twitch like a memory
forgotten bars
one of those cities
one of those nights
everyone's darling
everyone's sweetheart
just this drink to hold my hand
one glass of anything, anything cheap
and I'm here just because
everyone else has come just to be seen

Oh, I don't know these buildings
I think I'm lost

In the perfumed armpit of town
developed but dead now
these people are bricks
six faced stones wrapped up and bowed
such disappointment when the paper is ripped
so I stand, still boring and bored
itching my eye again against a wall

At the end, at the close
would you be good enough to take me home?
'Cause I don't know these buildings
I think I am lost
'cause I don't know these buildings
I think I am lost

Would you, would you
would you be good enough to take me home?
Would you, would you
would you be good enough to take me home?
Would you, would you
would you be good enough to take me home?
Would you, would you
would you be good enough to take me home?

"T H E   W O R K"

(with Archie Fisher)

Do the years add up
to the suck and the blow
of a breath and a beating heart?
There must be more

You can wash your face
with a sunset song
the lines will still remain
they'll never be gone

Will you bully your land
with a furrowed brow?
But King Harvest leaves
with a thinning crown

You may bow your head
as the hair recedes
but it's filled with years
that no one can steal

When the work stops working
what was light becomes a weight
when the work stops working
shall we pack it all in?
When the work stops working
and the weight becomes an ache
when the work stops working
shall we pack it all in
or start again?

Ah, the search for answers
is an idiot's task
I'm not halfway there
but don't want to ask

The search gives a glint
to the older eye
and I'll keep on looking
'til the day I die

618-1618516/03

Is the work half-worth it
when your hands grow raw?
When your knees keep creaking
like an old barn door

The gloves of love
become an old man's friend
and you've learned to make a stand
not to stoop and bend

When the work stops working
what was light becomes a weight
when the work stops working
shall we pack it all in?
When the work stops working
and the weight becomes an ache
when the work stops working
shall we pack it all in
or start again?

The lines remain
and they will never be gone
all life is filled with years
no one can steal
I'll keep on looking
'til the day I die
I'll learn to make a stand
not stoop and bend

When the work stops working
what was light becomes a weight
when the work stops working
shall we pack it all in?
When the work stops working
and the weight becomes an ache
when the work stops working
shall we pack it all in
or start again?

S: DO THE YEARS ADD UP TO ~~JUST~~ THE SUCK & BLOW
TO A ~~BEAT~~ & A ~~BREATH~~, THERE MUST BE MORE
Breath and beating heart

A: YOU CAN WASH YOUR FACE AT THE SUNSET'S SONG
~~BUT~~ THE LINES REMAIN, OH THEY'LL NEVER BE GONE

S: YOU BULLY YOUR LAND WITH A FURROWED BROW
BUT KING HARVEST LEAVES WITH A THINNING CROWN
You may bow your head

A: ~~YOUR~~ *life* ~~HEAD~~ ~~MAY~~ ~~FALL~~ AS THE HAIR RECEDES
I ~~BUT~~ IT'S FILLED WITH YEARS, THAT NO ONE CAN STEAL

WHEN THE WORK STOPS WORKING
~~AND~~ WHAT WAS LIGHT BECOMES A WEIGHT
WHEN THE WORK STOPS WORKING
Shall ~~DO~~ WE PACK IT ALL IN?
WHEN THE WORK STOPS WORKING
AND THE WEIGHT TURNS TO AN ACHE.
WHEN THE WORK STOPS WORKING
SHALL WE PACK IT ALL IN,
~~OR START AGAIN?~~

or start again —

A: ~~AND~~ THE SEARCHING GIVES ~~KEEPS~~ THE GLINT TO ~~AN~~ OLDER ~~~~ EYE

AND I'LL keep on LOOKING UNTIL THE ~~DAY~~ I DIE

S: IS THE WORK HALF WORTH IT WHEN YOUR

WHEN YOUR knees keep ~~KNEECAPS~~ CREAKY LIKE AN OLD ~~~~ BARN DOOR HANDS GROW RAW

A. The gloves of love soon become an old monofriend

And you'll learn to ~~~~ make a stand, not to stoop to bend

REF	618-198516.
ARTIST	FRIGHTENED RABBIT
TITLE	"State Hospital EP"
MONTH / YEAR	SEPT 2 4 2012

"STATE HOSPITAL"

The half-backflip conception
state hospital birth
the most threadbare, tall story
the country has ever heard
brought home to breathe smoke
in the arms of her mother
the blunt kitchen knife
who just lays in a submissive position
beneath a national weight
and the slow arc of a fist

Her heart beats like a breezeblock
thrown down the stairs
her blood is thicker than concrete
forced to be brave, she was
born into a grave

And in the limp three years of bored schooling
she's accustomed to hearing that she could never run far
a slipped disc in the spine of community
a bloody curse word in a pedestrian verse
spirits in graveyards and fingers in car parks
she cries on the high street just to be heard
a screaming anchor for nothing in particular
at the foot of the fuck of it
dragging her heels in the dirt

Her heart beats like a breezeblock
thrown down the stairs
her blood is thicker than concrete
forced to be brave, she was
born into a grave

The cheek of youth flashed red and turned grey
now she lies on the pavement she is helped to her feet
all thighs, hair and magpie handbags
Saturday's uniform for the 'fuck me' parade
brought home to keep warm

in the arms of a plumber, ruddy and balding
who just needs a spine to dig in to
a chest for the head and a hand for the holding

Her heart beats like a breezeblock
thrown down the stairs
her blood is thicker than concrete
forced to be brave, she was, she was...

Her heart beats like a breezeblock
thrown down the stairs
her skin is thicker than concrete
forced to be brave, she was, she was...

A broken elevator anthem
held between floors
but if blood is thicker than concrete
all is not lost
all is not lost
all is not lost
all is not lost.

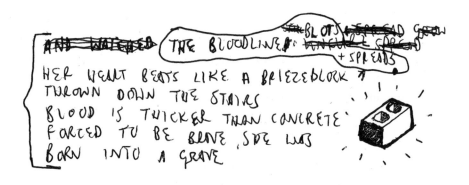

618-198516/01

"BOXING NIGHT"

Boxing Night
I celebrate in style
in boxer shorts and spirits
floor littered with ghosts of bottles past

There's a naked hush
clothed only in breath and the pulse
of a heart that is kicking
as though it is desperate to be born

I am hostage blind
deaf to the din outside
good Glasgow could burn to it's timber tonight
I'd barely blink an eye

Well, the clock just stopped
you can cut that into my headstone
won't something move so I stop
staring a hole into the phone

You can get me at home
with a drink to ill-health
just me and these walls
and a beaten-up chair
on Boxing Day

This is Boxing Night
someone lost an eye
I swear I've lost the last drop
of whatever kept me awake, alive

I fell in the fourth from a heavy right hook
to a blushed and swollen face
in a single blow it's murdered
then it takes years to waste away

I can't call you all mine anymore
I can't call you full stop

but you know you can call me up anytime
call me whatever the fuck you want

You can get me at home
with a drink to ill-health
just me and these walls and a beaten-up chair
You can get me at home
with a drink to ill-health
just me and these walls
and a beaten-up chair
on Boxing Day.

618-198516/02

"HOME FROM WAR"

Here I stand like a soldier, home from war
with nothing to do but remember the shudder of bombs
I'm sure it never quite goes away
it never quite goes away

Here I sit like a beginner, beginning again
all those fuckups counted for nothing, 'cause nothing
makes sense
and I am never quite fully awake
and never completely asleep, yeah

I'm walking around like a soldier who's home from war
lost in a foreign landscape I used to know
and will I ever feel like I belong?
Will I ever feel like I belong anywhere?

Here I lie like a lover who isn't in love
who stares at the cracks in the ceiling 6-feet above
and he knows just how it feels
to buckle beneath the weight
there is only so much he can take
only so much he can take

I might never be normal again
I might never be normal again
never be normal again
never be normal again
but who cares?
I ask, who cares? who cares?

Now I'm standing dishevelled, at your door
covered in dust and dirt, but full of hope
and we might never be normal again
we might never be normal again
but who cares?
I ask, who cares?

618-198516/03

"OFF"

We'll have no telephones here
just a gentle mouth to a smitten ear
no technology here
such heady chemistry can't be engineered
we'll use no binary code
no pixelate template to contain us both
ignore the scurrying roads
we will stay right here and want for nothing more

And as the earth eats itself
swallows us whole
we will sever ourselves
switch everything off

No machinery here
no chain-smoking factories with their monotone sneer
no technology here
no damning indictments or digital sin
so can't we both disappear?
Run away and play dead like I did last year
we'll need nobody else at all
sheltered and happy in our candlelit home

And as the earth eats itself
swallows us whole
we can lie here hidden
pull the wires from the wall
oh, as the earth eats itself
swallows us whole
we will sever ourselves
switch everything off.

"WEDDING GLOVES"

(with Aidan Moffat)

A melting of morals
a solder of souls
as sexy as lace
but with just as much holes
doubts were debated
and questions were raised
all the stags and the hens
were stunned and amazed
the portents and omens rang as loud as the bells
with you at the altar
and me in the cells

Are you still breathing?
Are you holding it in?
Was it you I heard sniffing
when you were stooped at the sink?
Are we still breathing?
Or are we holding it in?
After all of this swimming
are we beginning to sink?

The dress will decay
but be in no doubt
you can scrub, you can soak
but you can't wash me out
you can call it perversion
you can call it a kink
but no one could see us
there's no need to think

Are you still breathing?
Are you holding it in?
Was it you I heard sniffing
when you were stooped at the sink?
Are we still breathing?
Or are we holding it in?
After all of this swimming
are we beginning to sink?

All of these old stains
all of them ours
anniversary fingerprints
scattered all through the house
do you even remember
what we said in the vows?
God was watching one Saturday
but he is not with us now, with us now

Turn away from me darling
face to the wall.
turn the big light out
I've locked the front door
squeeze on the wedding gloves
your hands to the wall
it's the only posterity
you will grant me at all, grant me at all

Grip me in your wedding glove
fake silk touch to my face
tens of years of giddy love
come rushing back again.

Grip me in your wedding glove
fake silk touch to my face
tens of years of giddy love
come rushing back again.

PEDESTRIAN VERSE

REF	
	618-1622.
ARTIST	FRIGHTENED RABBIT
TITLE	
	"Pedestrian Verse"
MONTH / YEAR	
	FEB 4 2013

WE'LL CROWD ROUND THIS COWERING BODY
& ~~BARK~~ & BARK ~~UNTIL ITS~~ ~~UNTIL~~ TURN
~~FROM~~ ~~THICK FINGERS~~ ~~FAINT~~ THICK FINGERS, ~~THICK STONES~~ ~~THREE FINE~~
~~LET~~ PROMISE ~~TO THE~~ TO THE ~~STICKS~~ ~~STICKS~~ STICKS
~~FEEL~~ ~~FEEL~~ ~~THAT~~ GIRLS WE ~~MARRIED~~ MARRIED & STONES
WE'LL LOVE THEM, THOUGH WE ~~ALWAYS~~ PROBABLY ~~DON'T~~ WON'T

~~I WILL GOVERN~~
MAN ~~HE~~ HE
~~BUT~~ ~~WE~~ ~~MAN SHIT~~ EVEN LAUGH ~~EVER~~
~~THEY~~ ~~THE~~ BREEDS ~~SHOULDN'T~~ ~~CHANGE~~ ~~THEY~~ SHOULDN'T
~~SCALE~~ ~~&~~ BREED~~ING~~ ~~THEIR~~ JUST BECAUSE ~~THEY~~ COMES
~~ACT THE~~ HEY
~~BE~~ A FATHER FOR A WEEK OR SO
~~& SHOULD~~ ~~THEN~~ ~~GO BACK TO BEING A CUNT~~
~~THEN GO BACK TO BEING A CUNT~~
UNTIL ~~THEIR~~ WORST INSTINCTS RETURN
~~ANY ONE OF US COULD BE ONE OF THESE MEN~~

~~FORE~~ ~~ARE~~ ~~SEE~~ S
IDLE, SLOW & AND SCARED
~~TOO~~ ~~INVISIBLE~~ ~~WITH FEAR~~
~~TEN~~
~~ARE~~ ~~HEROIC~~ ACTS OF MAN
~~FOR~~ ~~OF~~
AS I ~~FROM HERE~~ SIT
I'LL JUST WATCH ~~FROM~~ ~~OVER HERE~~
HEROIC ACTS OF MAN

BORED, ~~SLIGHTLY SHAKED~~, ~~SO~~

I'M HERE. I'M HERE. NOT HEROIC
BUT I TRY

~~& SEES~~ ~~WITH A BENT~~
WHILE
~~& SEES~~ A KNIGHT IN SHITTY ARMOUR
ONE MAN SQUARES UP TO
~~ACETERAT~~ TEARS INTO ~~THE~~
~~LOVER~~ INTRUDER

RIPS ~~DANCER~~
A DRINKER
~~BARE FACE~~ BANCER FROM ~~HER~~
DAMSEL ~~IN A DRESS~~ IN A DRESS
DRUNK OUT ~~FROM~~ HER
LION'S
DRINK LOVE? ~~POURED~~ ~~& PUFFIN~~
~~CHEATING~~
WIDE COWARD'S HEARTS IN ~~& PUFFIN~~ CREEPS

"ACTS OF MAN"

I am that dickhead in the kitchen
giving wine to your best girl's glass
I am the amateur pornographer
unpleasant publisher by hand

Not here, not here
heroic acts of man

See the stumbling pinstripe trouser
the flecks of sick on an office shoe
part of the fatty British average
that lives in the houses around you

Not here, not here
heroic acts of man

Let's all crowd round the cowering body
throw stocky fingers, bricks and stones
let's promise every girl we marry
we'll always love them, when we probably won't
while a knight in shitty armour
rips a drunk out of her dress
one man tears into another
hides a coward's heart in a lion's chest

Man, he breeds although he shouldn't
he's breeding just because he comes
acts the father for a minute
until the worst instincts return

Not here, not here
heroic acts of man

I have never wanted more to be your man
and build a house around you
but I am just like all the rest of them
sorry, selfish, trying to improve

I'm here, I'm here
not heroic but I try.

"BACKYARD SKULLS"

All our secrets are smothered in dirt
underneath paving stones
lying, waiting to be told
some stay hidden, whilst some get found
like a long-lost soul
like a skull beneath the ground

Backyard skulls
deep beneath the ground
all those backyard skulls
are not deep enough to never be found

Here lies the first time that I was wrong
and there is still no sign
no exes mark this spot
of the ancient encounters
with foreign skin, all but perished by now
but you can't erase the grin from those

Backyard skulls
deep beneath the ground
those backyard skulls
are not deep enough to never be found

Through patio doors
lies century upon century
of skulls untold
hushed as suburban adultery
below our homes
and underneath the lawns we keep
white silent skulls
are smiling at the hypocrisy

Backyard skulls
deep beneath the ground
those backyard skulls
are not deep enough to never be found

Backyard skulls
deep beneath the ground
those backyard skulls
are not deep enough to never be found
deep enough to never be found
deep enough to never be found

BACKYARD SKULLS

ALL OUR SECRETS, ~~SMOTHERED~~ ~~CLOSED~~ IN ~~DIRT~~ ~~EARTH~~

LIE ~~BURIED~~ COVERED BY PAVING STONES

~~LYING~~ ~~WAITING~~ TO BE TOLD

THOUGH ~~SOME~~ ~~RELIGIOUS~~ STAY HIDDEN

~~(SO~~ ~~SECRETS ARE~~ ~~SOME GET FOUND)~~

LIKE ~~SOME~~ LONG LOST SOUL

LIKE A ~~EMPTY~~ ~~SKULL~~ BENEATH THE GROUND

~~OH~~

~~ALL~~ THESE BACKYARD SKULLS

DEEP BENEATH THE GROUND

BACKYARD SKULLS

NOT DEEP ENOUGH TO NEVER BE FOUND

ANCIENT ~~BITTER~~ ENCOUNTERS ~~WITH~~ ~~SKIN AGAINST~~ /SKIN

~~LUST~~ ~~&~~ FOREIGN ~~BODIES~~ ~~FOREIGN TONGUES~~

~~KEY~~ ~~BE~~ ~~SILENT~~ ~~SILENCE~~ ~~HAVE~~ HAVE PERISHED NOW BY

~~ALL BUT~~

BUT ~~HOW YOU LOVED~~ ~~ZIPPED IN~~ ~~BODY~~ PLASTIC BAGS

~~I'LL~~ ~~YOU'LL~~ NEVER ~~ERASE~~ ~~FORGET~~

CAN'T ESCAPE THE GRIN ~~OF~~ ~~ON FROM~~ THOSE

BACKYARD SKULLS

HERE LIES THE FIRST TIME THAT

I ~~WAS~~ ~~WRONG~~ ~~TOLD A LIE~~ ~~DID~~ ~~WAS~~ WRONG

AND ~~YET~~ THERE'S (STILL) IS NO SIGN.

~~NO SIGNS~~

NOTHING MARK(S) THE SPOT OF ~~THOSE~~

MINOR KEY
1BREAK DOWN
?

✝ "HOLY" ✝
- - - -

While you read to me from the riot act
way on high
clutching a crisp New Testament
breathing fire
will you save me the fake benevolence?
I don't have time
I'm just too far gone for a telling
I've lost my pride

I don't mind being lonely
so leave me alone
you're acting all holy
me, I'm just full of holes

I could dip my head in the river
cleanse my soul
I'd still have the stomach of a sinner
face like an un-holy ghost
will you save me all the soliloquies?
I've paid my fines
I'll be gone before my deliverance
preach what you like

I don't mind being lonely
so leave me alone
you're acting all holy
me, I'm just full of holes, full of holes

Don't mind being lonely
so spare me the brimstone
acting all holy
when you know I'm full of holes
don't mind being lonely
don't need to be told
stop acting so holy
I know I'm full of holes, full of holes

I don't mind being lonely
won't you leave me alone?
You're oh so holy
and I'll never be good enough
don't care if I'm lonely
'cause this feels like home
and I'll never be holy
thank God I'm full of holes
full of holes.

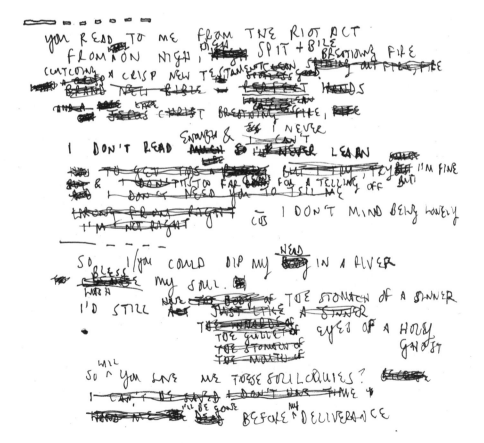

THE WOODPILE (OVER ACOUSTIC - CLASSICAL)

Will you come back to my corner?
Spent too long alone tonight
Will you come brighten my corner
LIKE → A lit torch to the woodpile.

Come find me, where I hide
We'll speak in our secret tongue.

FAR FROM THE ELECTRIC FLOOR
REMOVED FROM THE RED MEAT MARKET
I SEARCH FOR A FIRE DOOR
AN ESCAPE FROM THE DRUMS & BARKING

BEREFT OF ALL SOCIAL CHARM
CAST OUT BY MY OWN ADMISSION
• I FALL INTO A CORNER'S ARMS
~~THEY ARE BEST TO GO MISSING~~
THEY SO HARD ~~JUST~~ TO GO MISSING

YOU'RE ~~XXX~~ MILES FROM THE ~~NIGHTCLUB~~ DARKENED SMOKE
LIGHT YEARS FROM THE BLACK ~~XXXX~~ ~~LATE NIGHT~~
~~XXX~~ SUBURBS ~~MIDNIGHT~~ ~~BRIGHT PINK~~

IN ~~A HOTEL~~ HOTEL ROOM, I
~~STRIVE TO~~ ~~FAIL~~ ALONE

BOOK O' MATCHES / DEADWOOD
POUR PETROL, STRIKE & TURN,

"THE WOODPILE"

Far from the electric floor
removed from the red meat market
I look for a fire door
an escape from the drums and barking
bereft of all social charms
struck dumb by the hand of fear
I fall into the corner's arms
the same way that I've done for years
I'm trapped in a collapsing building
come find me now, where I hide and
we'll speak in our secret tongues

Will you come back to my corner?
Spent too long alone tonight.
Would you come and brighten my corner?
A lit torch to the woodpile, aye

Dead wood waits to ignite
there's no spark on a dampened floor
a snapped limb in an unlit pyre
won't you come and break down this door?
I'm trapped in an abandoned building
come find me now, where I hide and
we'll speak in our secret tongues

Will you come back to my corner?
Spent too long alone tonight.
would you come and brighten my corner?
A lit torch to the woodpile, aye

Come find me now, where I hide and
we'll speak in our secret tongues.

"LATE MARCH, DEATH MARCH"

I cursed in church again and the handclaps all fell quiet
I watched a statue of you cry
a candle is blown, so we start the black march home
through a stale and silent night

There's a funeral in your eyes, and a drunk priest
at your side
staggering sermons never wash
there's no reproach from a lit touch paper,
both got stubborn marrow in bastard bones

Can we just get home, sleep this off?
Throw some 'sorrys' and then do it all again, well?

Folded arms clutch homicide
the bridge is out and the river's high
this is a March, Death! March!
March, Death! March!
There isn't a God, so I'll save my breath
pray silence for the road ahead
in this March, Death! March!
March, Death! March!
I went too far

And as we walk through an hour long pregnant pause
no grain of truce can be born
my bridge is burned and perhaps we'll shortly learn
that it was arson all along

Shall we just get home, sleep this off?
Throw some 'sorrys' and then do it all again?
Well, like Bulver said, less heart and more head
so un-furrow that brow, un-plant those seeds of doubt oh

Folded arms clutch homicide
the bridge is out and the river's high
In this March, Death! March!
March, Death! March!

618-1622/05

There isn't a God, so I'll save my breath
pray silence for the road ahead
in this March, Death! March!
March, Death! March!
Dead balloons and withered flowers
sorry cannot save me now
in this March, Death! March!
March, Death! March!
Think I went too far.

¿SHAKE YR CROSS?

(SO SHAKE ~~your~~ CROSS) TIL THE CHRIST FALLS OFF
(SHAKE YR HEAD) ~~Till you~~ ~~SNAP~~ CLACK ~~THAT~~ ~~BREAK~~ NECK

SING   LAAAAAAA-DAAA-DAAA-DAAA (etc)

"DECEMBER'S TRADITIONS"

December's traditions
suck the last of summer from our cheeks
draws the curtains, strips the trees
in so-called living rooms
Scottish pastimes come to roost
love's labour stain a linen sheet

The ghostly body
who makes his bed beside you
is slowly losing teeth
the boy needs sunlight
and a shot of modesty
he needs to get some sleep

It's not the answer
a sticking plaster on a shattered bone
what do you need?
What do you need from me?
It's not the answer
treating cancer like a cold
what do you need?
What do you need from me?

After months of grieving
fuck the grief, I'm leaving
will you leave with me?
The blood loss, the towering cost
of mouth to mouth and tongue to tongue
one lick brings warm metallic taste
I can correct myself
convince you that there's no-one else
in volumes of new leaves
if you want a saint, you don't want me

It's not the answer
a sticking plaster on a shattered bone
what do you need?
What do you need from me?

It's not the answer
treating cancer like a cold
what do you need?
What do you need from me?
It's not the answer
I'm just begging to be told
what do you need?
What do you need from me?
If I had the answer
I'd write a book on what I know
what do you need?
What do you need from me?

IT'S   NOT THE ANSWER
A STICKING PLASTER ON A SHATTERED BONE
WHAT DO YOU NEED? WHAT DO YOU NEED FROM ME?
IT'S   NOT THE ANSWER
TO KEEP TREATING CANCER LIKE A COLD
WHAT DO YOU NEED? WHAT DO YOU NEED FROM
                                    ME.
PLEASE FORGIVE MY MACRO FAME
I AM BEGGING TO BE TOLD
WHAT DO YOU NEED

"HOUSING (IN)"

Hear the dull drum roll
of the Great North Eastern line's
coupled carriage ticking like
my metronome
and see that housing glow
a skyline of cheap gold
and crooked teeth I will call home
for a day or so

You can't carry me away now
please don't steal me from my house
you can't carry me away now
I have just laid my head down
you can't carry me away now
please don't steal me from my house
you can't carry me, don't steal me from my house

Inside that housing glow
I stiffen my tired shoes
with the starch of family food
oh, I've missed you so

You can't carry me away now
please don't steal me from my house
you can't carry me away now
I have just laid my head down
you can't carry me away now
please don't steal me from my house
you can't carry me, don't steal me from my house.

618-1622/07

"DEAD NOW"

I am not myself I am
a broken boxer stuffed with glass and sand
this is not how health should feel
songs sung from the lungs of the elderly

I'm dead now, check my chest and you'll see
the life has been mined from me, burned for the heat
I'm dead now, can you hear the relief
as life's belligerent symphonies finally cease

I put my heart where my mouth is
now I can't thumb it down again
I've gone devilled my kidneys
now he's living inside of me
so if we can't bring an exorcist
I'll settle for one of your stiffest drinks
and we'll scream hell towards heaven's door
and I will piss on your front porch

I'm dead now, check my chest and you'll see
the life has been mined from me, burned for the heat
I'm dead now, can you hear the relief
as life's belligerent symphonies finally cease
we're all dead now, join hands and we'll sing
to the glory of hell and the virtue of sin

There's something wrong with me...
There's something wrong with me...

There is something wrong with me
and it reads nothing like poetry
so will you love me spite of these
tics and inconsistencies?
There is something wrong with me.

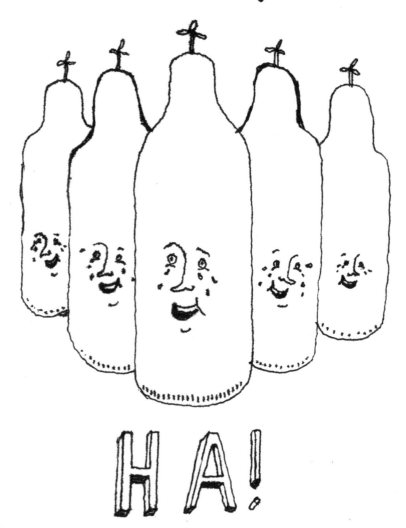

"NITROUS GAS"

Shut down the gospel singers
and turn up the old heartbreakers
I'm dying to tell you that I'm dying here

Throw up the sickly joy and I'll
swallow the sweet self-loathing
I'm just dying to be unhappy again

Oh, where love won't grow
Oh, I'll build my home
but if happiness won't come to me
hand me the nitrous gas

Leave the acute warm-heartedness
go where the joyless bastard lives
he's dying to bring you down with him

Suck in the bright red major key
spit out the blue minor misery
I'm dying to bring you down with me

but if happiness won't come to me
hand me the nitrous gas
you can keep all of your oxygen
hand me the nitrous gas
if happiness won't live with me
I think I can live with that
you can keep all of your oxygen
hand me the nitrous gas.

"HOUSING (OUT)"

I've been taken again
kidnapped before dawn
stolen by these songs
oh damn them all

Beyond the housing glow
looking back will lose its point
so stare forward into the void
of the endless road

You can't carry me away now
please don't steal me from my house
you can't carry me away now
I have just laid my head down
you can't carry me away now
please don't steal me from my house
you can't carry me, don't steal me from my house.

"THE OIL SLICK"

I went looking for a song for you
something soft and patient to reflect its muse
I took a walk with all my brightest thoughts
but the weather soon turned and they all ran off
took to the ocean, in a boat this time
only an idiot would swim through the shit I write
how can I talk of light and warmth?
I've got a voice like a gutter in a toxic storm

All the dark words pouring from my throat
sound like an oil slick coating the wings we've grown
there goes a love song drifting out to sea
I'd sing along if I could hear over the oil slick

So it came to pass and I came home
with four worn out limbs and not one love song
how predictable, this is all you've got
yet another selfish signpost to my ruin of faults

All the dark words pouring from my throat
sound like an oil slick coating the wings we've grown
there goes a love song drifting out to sea
I'd sing along if I could hear
over the dark words pissing from my throat
sound like an oil slick coating the wings we've grown
there goes a love song drifting out of my reach
I'd sing along if I could see past the oil slick

There is light but there's a tunnel to crawl through
there is love but its misery loves you
there's still hope so I think we'll be fine
in these disastrous times, disastrous times
there is light but there's a tunnel to crawl through
there is love but its misery loves you
we've still got hope so I think we'll be fine
in these disastrous times, disastrous times.

618-1622/12

"IF YOU WERE ME"

Time passes, I accept the blame
and I accept that you might never care to see me again
at least I can shake off some shame
still I quiver like a dying leaf in a violent wind

I don't wish to be excused for this
my disguise and my excuses they had worn so thin
but may I ask and answer honestly
what would you have done if you were me?

How could it go so wrong so quickly?
What would you do if you were me?
Don't assume that I have found this easy
how would you feel if you were me?

Time passes and kills everything
in its path and then it buries us in history
but some bits, some bits seem to stick
oh I thought that you and I could be a timeless thing

I have to ask, please answer honestly
what would you have done if you were me?

How could it go so wrong so quickly?
What would you do if you were me?
Don't assume that I have found this easy
how would you feel if you were me?

"SNOW STILL MELTING"

We're ruled by a governing frost
it melts beneath alcohol briefly
and then bites back
we breathe on panes of glass
a circle appears before freezing again
and it's taking its time
degree by reluctant degree
and night by night

The snow is still melting, and doesn't it take its time?

We're ruled by a governing frost
it's as thin as a wedding veil
too heavy to lift for a kiss
and a kiss brings warmth
but not nearly enough to finish the thaw
and call spring from six months in clothes
this calls for bold, naked honesty
petrol, a match and a torch

The snow is still melting, and doesn't it take its time?
To have lost almost all feeling, Jesus, didn't that take
a while?

Well, the snow may have melted but it covered all kinds
of dirt
we can take one brush each, start sweeping and we'll
clear this up
oh, the snow may have melted but it covered all
kinds of hurt
if we take one brush each, start sweeping and we'll
clear this up
clear this up.

"ESCAPE ROUTE"

His first kicking came on January 1st
they said, "Welcome to the club,
we'll take your shoes and your shirt"
He wore his nosebleed like a red rosette
and it was a prize he would win again and again
and again

He had to find an escape route

It was a rumour, that soon became true
when he was drunk in the suburbs
with a boy from a different school
all his good friends soon left him for dead
and now he stands staring down at the Clyde from
a bridge

And then he saw an escape route
from the dogs of West Renfrew
from the bitches and bruises
he chose Ohio to run to

The name came to him just as he perched
on the amber-lit bridge, his whole face pursed
it had a ring to it in American songs
as a glittering release from this crippling curse
he dreamt of the place of a cinematic space
and all the pointing fingers they just melted away
well who knows, maybe he'll never take flight
but he swears Ohio pulled him from the bridge that night

It became an escape route
from the dogs of West Renfrew
from the bitches and beatings
Midwestern chest to fall into

Some are saved by the good arms
some are saved by the church
some get saved by the skin of their teeth

by the thought that it couldn't get much worse
some are saved by professors
some are saved by police
some get saved by a distant place
by an impossible American dream

We all need an escape route

We all need an escape route
from the punches and kicks
the fingernails and the pricks
all the sharp little knives
in the dark pockets of life
from the bitches and bruises
from the burden of youth
the public hangings and stonings
save us from fellow humans
just give us an escape route.

REF	618-1622219.
ARTIST	FRIGHTENED RABBIT
TITLE	"Pedestrian Verse" Singles & B-Sides
MONTH / YEAR	~~XXXXXX~~ 2012/2013

"TODAY'S CROSS"

Today's cross stung like a bit bottom lip
drew no blood
sucked like a desperate kiss

Today's cross, such an amateur bitch
it's made of three nails, two sticks and a ball of string
it's three nails, two sticks ...

Keep me close, like best enemies
just a little closer now, for that shoe shining
keep me close, like best enemies
just a little closer now, for that shoe shining

Today's cross had such a cowardly bark
today's cross only left an elastic mark
today's cross, it had holes in its holes
its dick in its fist, oh and doesn't it show?
it's made of three nails, two sticks and a ball of string

Don't go
need you right now
don't go
I need your right hand

Keep me close, like best enemies
just a little closer now, for that shoe shining
keep me close, like best enemies
just a little closer now, for that shoe shining
keep me close, like best enemies
just a little closer now, for that shoe shining
keep me close like best enemies
just a little closer now, there's that shoe shining.

"ARCHITECT"

(with Andy Hull)

Don't waste your time on me
I'm just an architect
I have built nothing
please take my arms in assistance
if I offer them
I can salve that sting
your life held in low regard
beneath low ceilings
they are designed by fate
tonight we can tear the roof
from this existence
I'll tear it all away

You told all of your friends
you told all of your friends
told all of your friends
and no one came
no one came

You claimed my device is an arsonist
just burn in time
you say that it won't show light
just a darkening
a waste of time
you shaved bits of spine from a novelist
to help you write
you say and there's nothing here
but a masochist
and a broken mind

You told all of your friends
you told all of your friends
you told all of your friends
and no one came
no one came

They didn't want to
no one came
they didn't have to
oh, no one came
they didn't need to
oh, no one came
they didn't want to
no one came
no one came.

          618-1622219/02

"DEFAULT BLUES"

Turn the polite dull ache to a shrieking pain
turn that hair into a haircut and change your name
through yellow teeth white lies are told
of the notches made and the ounces of smoke

So, pick the padlock case in the padlocked room
wipe the smile from your face and sing the
default blues, it goes...

What are you running from ah ha?
What are you running from ah?
The past may die but it's never gone
what are you running from ah?

This is textbook heartbreak from the country school
a prescription sculpture of a thoughtless stool
you've got your heroin monologues that you lifted
from books
now you're wearing a helmet whilst you're breaking
the rules

Pick the padlocked case in the padlocked room
wipe the smile from your face and sing the
default blues, it goes...

What are you running from ah ha?
What are you running from ah?
The past may die but it's never gone
what are you running from ah?
What are you running from ah ha?
What are you running from ah?
The accent you hid behind is gone
what are you running from?

There isn't a cure
There isn't a cure
There isn't a cure...

So, save your waxwork torture for your modelling friends
it's fake emotional trash raked from Zimmermann's bin

Pick the padlocked case in the padlocked room
wipe the smile from your face and sing the default
blues, it goes...

What are you running from ah ha?
What are you running from ah?
The accent you hid behind is gone
what are you running from?

What are you running from ah ha?
What are you running from ah?
The past may die but it's never gone
what are you running from ah?

618-1622219/03

"RADIO SILENCE"

I speculate the quiet nights, how and where your
body lies
who owns the knee that clicks into the jigsaw piece that
I once knew?
And I could break the silence, but I fear I've held you
back enough
the space exists so time can tell, but so much space
becomes a cell

It's been so long since I heard you speak
one last click and a long, long bleep
then radio silence, radio silence
it's been too long since you turned that cheek
one last kiss on a faceless street
then radio silence, radio silence

Your voice is but an echo now, it whispers through my
haunted house
the burn has blistered up and healed, the scent of flesh
has disappeared
the crows have flown and left their shit, I've tried to
chip away at this
but now it seems I'm ill-prepared, the saddest songs are
all I hear

It's been so long since I heard you speak
one last click and a long, long bleep
then radio silence, radio silence
it's been too long since you turned that cheek
one last kiss on a faceless street
then radio silence, radio silence

It's been so long since I heard you speak
one last click then a long, long bleep
then radio silence, radio silence
it's been too long since you turned that cheek
one last kiss on a faceless street
then radio silence, radio silence

Radio silence
radio silence...

CANDLELIT ~~(THE PSYCHOPATH SONG)~~

[27.02.2013]

I WON'T GET IN LINE
I WILL NOT WAIT FOR THIS
WITH MY ~~JUST~~ BARE HANDS
I'D KILL ^JUST^ TO BE CANDLELIT
WITH YOU

LOOK AT THE BLOODBATH, DARLING
LOOK AT THE MESS I HAVE MADE
WITH MY BARE HANDS
I KILLED ~~I KILLED~~ JUST FOR BE CANDLELIT
WITH YOU

THE BOYS ARE IN FOR A BOTTLING

I AM ~~FINISHED~~ PLAYING ROCK, PAPER, SCISSORS
GONNA ~~TAKE~~ ^GRAB^ THAT ROCK & KNOCK 'EM ALL ~~DOWN~~ WITH IT
GRAB ~~THOSE~~ SCISSORS ~~AND~~ SLIT SOME THROATS
~~PUT~~ ~~A PEN~~ TO THE PAPER & WRITE A LOVE NOTE
~~PUSH A~~ ^A PEN ACROSS THE^ PAPER

I WON'T GET IN LINE
I WILL NOT WAIT FOR THIS
WITH MY ~~BARE~~ BARE HANDS I'D KILL TO BE
                                    CANDLELIT
WITH YOU......

THIS ~~THE~~ EARTH'S VIOLENT PAST ~~THESE~~ TEARING
IN ~~BOYS GRABS BUT~~ ~~MEN~~ WOULD ~~TRAVEL~~ FOR MILES & MILES
& MURDERED ~~ALL~~ ~~BOYS~~ ~~THEM~~ WHO TRIED TO ~~GET IN THEIR~~
BUT LOVE ALSO LOST ~~BEFORE~~ ~~THEN~~ ~~HALOUR~~ ~~OF ITS~~ ~~VIOLENT~~ ~~PAST~~ AND ~~GREATLY~~ COST ~~THEY~~
~~ONCE WHAT LOVE COULD COST AN ARMY OF LIVES~~
MAN ~~E~~ USED TO ~~THE~~ KNOW ~~A FIELD OF BLOOD~~

/ LOVE HAS A VIOLENT PAST
/ LITTERED WITH ^THE^ ~~TERRIBLE~~ ACTS OF REASONABLE MEN
ON THE HEADS THAT ROLLED, ~~AND THE JUST TO BE LAID~~
                              ON THE ~~RIBS~~ ~~THAT~~ BROKE
                                    RIBS THAT BROKE
~~GET IN THE NAME OF IT~~
~~JUST TO GET THE GIRL IN~~ IN THE NAME OF A GIRL

"CANDLELIT"

Love's checkered past
is littered with violent acts
and the blood that filled countless baths
each drop drawn in her name

In this modern age
the image of valour has changed
but I'm ready and willing to wage
a gut-wrenched war
for a minute of your time

I'm done playin' stone-paper-scissors
gonna grab that stone and bring 'em all down with it
steal those scissors and cut some throats
put pen to the paper and write you a note

I won't get in line
I will not wait for this
with my bare hands I'd kill
just to be candlelit
with you

I have no checkered past
I've never been a violent man
well, maybe you've changed all that
each scar I carve is in your name

So let suitors come
I can see them off, one by one
open every last artery up
just for a second of your time

Oh...

I'm done playin' stone-paper-scissors
gonna grab that stone and bring 'em all down with it
steal those scissors and cut some throats
put pen to the paper and I'll write you a note

I won't get in line
I will not wait for this
with my bare hands I'd kill
just for the privilege

Look at the blood bath
look at the mess I have made
with my bare hands I'd kill
just to be candlelit
with you

Oh I'd kill for one
I'd kill for one night candlelit
I'd kill for one
I'd kill for one night candlelit.

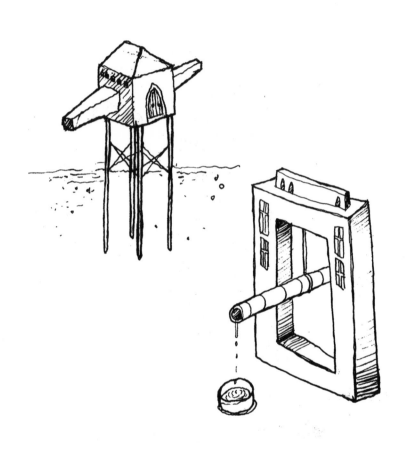

REF

618-16151161.

ARTIST

FRIGHTENED RABBIT

TITLE

"Painting Of A
Panic Attack"

MONTH / YEAR

APR 8 2016

"DEATH DREAM"

It was dawn and the kitchen light was still on,
I stepped in and found a suicide asleep on the floor
an open mouth, screams and makes no sound
apart from the ring of the tinnitus of silence
you had your ear to the ground

White noise.
I don't know if there's breathing or not,
butterflied arms, tell me that this one has flown
blood seems black against the skin on your
porcelain back
a still life is the last I will see of you,
my painting of a panic attack

You died in my sleep last night...

Death dreams I don't forget,
it's been a while since I dreamed this
even now when I sleep, I tread with care.

618-16151161/01

"GET OUT"

I'm in the arch of the church
between her thumb and her forefinger
I'm a worshipper
a zealot king, cursed
a devotee of the heady golden dance she does
she's an uncut drug
I found a vein and a pulse
chased it and for a minute I was floating dead
above myself

Get out of my heart
she won't, she won't
get out of my heart
she won't, she won't
I saw a glimmer in the dark
and now I know
she won't get out of my heart
she won't

I'm in your purse, pull me out, throw me down
stick me to your lip and draw a scarlet 'O'
there's a name on my chest in red
the embossing of a branded bull
I don't want you to

Get out of my heart
she won't, she won't
get out of my heart
she won't, she won't
I saw a glimmer in the dark
and now I know
she won't get out of my heart
she won't

Get out of my heart
she won't, she won't
get out of my heart
she won't, she won't
There's a heavenly scar
it lets me know
she won't get out of my heart
she won't.

"I WISH I WAS SOBER"

Fall prey to the blizzard head
I wrap my hand around the glass again
we all thought that I might change as I got older
fell down and nothing bled
wrapped in cotton alcohol again
"To the hilt!" I hear from the prick up on my shoulder
free pour the fruitless thought
far too late to talk so much but
still not giving up, though I wish that I was sober

Forgive me, I can't speak straight
forgive me, I can't...
forgive me, it's far too late

Choke down the gateway drug
open the gates in came the flood, it comes
like a blush of love it hits me without warning
long nights of getting lost
I walk beneath a bridge I don't know
I need a black suit, for tomorrow I'm in mourning
my love, you should know
the best of me left hours ago so
shove a rag into my mouth and let me smoulder
the fallout and the damage done
I can't un-sink the things I've sunk
still not giving up, though I wish that I was sober

Forgive me, I can't speak straight
forgive me, I can't...
forgive me, it's far too late

Come and shake me till I'm dry
I wish that I was sober
come to me and kill the night off
I wish that I was sober.

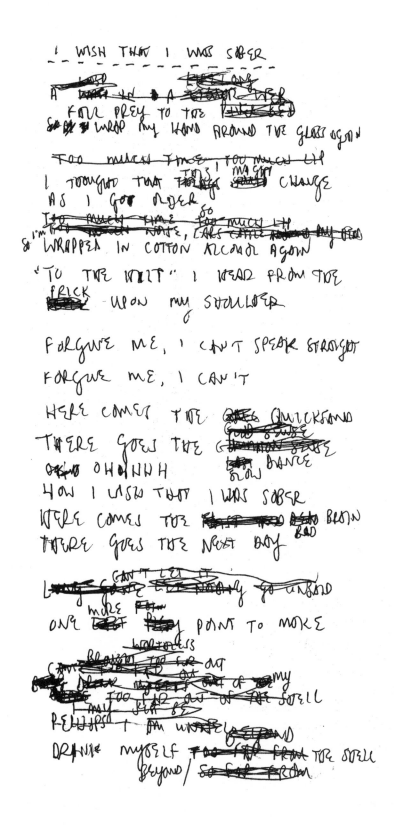

I WISH THAT I WAS SOBER

A ~~____~~ IN A ~~_____~~
FALL PREY TO THE ~~_____~~
~~____~~ WRAP MY HAND AROUND THE GLASS AGAIN

~~TOO MUCH TIME TOO MUCH LIP~~
I THOUGHT THAT ~~_____~~ CHANGE
AS I GOT OLDER
~~I TOO MUCH TIME TOO MUCH LIP~~
~~SO I'M ____ NOISE, LESS _____ MY ___~~
SO WRAPPED IN COTTON ALCOHOL AGAIN

"TO THE HILT" I READ FROM THE
~~BRICK~~ UPON MY SHOULDER

FORGIVE ME, I CAN'T SPEAK STRAIGHT

FORGIVE ME, I CAN'T

HERE COMES THE ~~____~~ QUICKSAND
THERE GOES THE ~~_____~~ SENSE
~~____~~ OHHHHH ~~____~~ DANCE
HOW I WISH THAT I WAS SOBER
HERE COMES THE ~~_____~~ BRAIN
THERE GOES THE NEXT BOY ~~BAD~~

~~_____~~ CAN'T LET IT ~~_____~~ GO UNSAID
ONE MORE ~~____~~ POINT TO MAKE
~~WORTHLESS~~
~~____ BLACKED TOO FAR OUT~~
~~_____ _____ _____ OUT OF MY~~
~~____ TOO FAR OUT OF THE SHELL~~
PERHAPS I AM UNRECLOSE~~____~~
DRANK MYSELF ~~____ ____~~ FROM THE SHELL
~~BEYOND/ SO FAR FROM~~

"WOKE UP HURTING"

Daybreak comes with the devil's hum
a carcass starts to breathe
wakes one more time to try and find
a place to count its teeth
and scrub the cuts from yesterday's
hot scuffle on the street
show me the door,
I need somewhere to go.

Daylight
woke up hurting
with tarmac to my side
I woke up with dirty knees
not for the first time
I woke up hurting
though I can't quite say why
I woke up hurting,
woke up hurting.

Slug through the day, sneak between
the houses I have made
and run sacred rivers up my sleeve
pills by mouth with lemonade
as the hours slow down, they all clock out
of the cracked up daily grind
I'm in a back back street, coming down
I wait for the beam of light
show me the door,
I need somewhere to go.

Midnight
woke up hurting
with tarmac to my side
I woke up with dirty knees
not for the first time
I woke up hurting
though I can't quite say why
I woke up hurting.

If all these southern tales are true
we should pray for abduction, pray it comes soon,
if all these southern tales are true
plan for Heaven though Hell will do.

"LITTLE DRUM"

I was mothered like an orchid
tethered to paternal sides
I hurried home in orbit
close to where I know I'm fine
no edge of the seat
no arms ever broken, you see

I waited for
the crash to come
too many days with
too little to do
I waited but
nothing came at all
so many days spent
in empty rooms

The little drum inside
behaves itself until you turn twenty-five
and then it strikes us all
we've lived this long but only ever half alive

I waited for
the crash to come
too many days with
too little to do
I waited but
nothing came at all
so many days spent
in empty rooms
it's too late for
a wasted youth
all quiet on the eastern front and
we dare not move
it's too late
to wage a war
so quiet on the eastern front and
we are all bored.

618-16151161/05

"STILL WANT TO BE HERE"

The perfect place
may never exist, may never exist
the perfect time
might be years and years away
the city is overweight
and it's pressing on the pair of us
we scowl and sweat
beneath the overbearing crush

But I still want to be here, want to be here
I still want to be here, want to be here
and I would live in a devil's ditch just to be near you
I still want to be here, want to be here

There is shit all over the street
outside our house now
junk veins dance at the bus stop
next to the rodeo clowns
nowhere to run to so
we hide like mislaid infants
fuck these faceless homes
and everyone who lives in them

But I still want to be here, want to be here
I still want to be here, want to be here
I would live in a shallow pit just to be near you
I still want to be here, want to be here

But I still want to be here, want to be here
I still want to be here, want to be here
and I would live in a devil's ditch just to be near you
I still want to be here.

I STILL WANT TO BE HERE

I still want to be here

~~I'd steal~~ ~~I'd~~

I would steal, I would

~~go~~ to be near you

The perfect ~~time~~ place

doesn't exist, doesn't exist

The perfect time is ~~always~~ always

a couple of days away

Bad luck shits on the ~~path~~

~~to~~ that we've been crawling down

~~The~~ ~~good times~~ ~~recovered~~

~~Lord above~~

The perfect place
may not exist, may not exist
The ~~perfect~~ time is ~~to~~
probably years & years away

There may be shit ~~all~~
all over the path that we've
been crawling down.

~~I don't care if I get~~
Shit ~~on my~~ hand ~~when~~
~~your~~ ~~around~~.

~~There~~ will be days when
~~we~~ get shit on ~~our~~ my hands

"AN OTHERWISE DISAPPOINTING LIFE"

I have a long list of tepid disappointments
it doesn't mention you
if I'm honest, your name could be upon it if this
didn't feel so good

In an otherwise disappointing life, made right
on an otherwise disappointing night, there's a fire
I don't need water, I just want to wave goodbye, goodbye
to an otherwise disappointing life

I took a pain pill to scrape a hole we could both
get lost in
cover love's bruise
so lay upon me and push until it's all forgotten
there are worse ways to lose you

In an otherwise disappointing life, made right
on an otherwise disappointing night, there's a fire
I don't need water, I just want to wave goodbye
and bring this otherwise disappointing life back to life

I have a long list of tepid disappointments
you should burn that too

In an otherwise disappointing life, you made right
on an otherwise disappointing night, there is a fire
in the hollow chapel suffering in silence
you're the choir
that sings this otherwise disappointing life back
to life.

618-16151161/07

"BREAK"

Took my bag underneath the overpass
forgot to bend and now I've broken all we have.
Nothing's worse than realising who you've hurt
I didn't bend and now we eat the consequence

Over the edge I can't stop myself
off the ledge throwing punches
over the edge I can't steer myself
all over again I don't want this

If I bend then I might not break
I should think about giving in
If I bend then I might be okay
If I think about how it ends
If I bend then I might not break
I should think about giving in
If I bend then I might be okay

Put down the bag in the calm before the aftermath
can we pick up all the debris of our bitter past?
Nothing's worse than realising who you've hurt
I didn't bend and now we eat the consequence

Over the edge I can't stop myself
off the ledge throwing punches
over the edge I can't steer myself
all over again I don't want this

If I bend then I might not break
I should think about giving in
If I bend then I might be okay
If I think about how it ends
If I bend then I might not break
I should think about giving in
If I bend then I might be okay
If I think about how it ends.

"BLOOD UNDER THE BRIDGE"

Clean out your mouth this is not what it's for
there's still a bloodstain from the spill of the war
pick up your sorrow this is not who we are
I won't cry, uncle, having come so far

It's alright, it's alright
it's just blood under the bridge
I'm too tired to fight
the affliction will be fixed.
It's alright, it's alright
it's just blood under the bridge
put down the knife and watch the
blood under the bridge go by

So tie your ragged fuck ups in a neat little knot
put it on the shelf behind the picture we bought
I've found a way to make the best of a flaw
and realise it's not the end it's an uncomfortable pause

It's alright, it's alright
it's just blood under the bridge
there is a fragment of light
but it's hiding in the distance.
It's alright, it's alright
it's just blood under the bridge
put down the knife and watch the
blood under the bridge go by

It's alright, it's alright
it's just blood under the bridge
I'm too tired to fight
and you're sick of feeling sick
so am I, but it's alright
it's just blood under the bridge
it's alright, it's alright
it's just blood under the bridge.

618-16151161/09

"400 BONES"

400 bones, crumpled in bed
I'm the only one who knows that you're still breathing
beneath the blanket of another French death
this afternoon is one I will be keeping
where skin is painted by a brush from the sun
pull the sheets up to your neck so she can't see us
and let the clocks do all the worrying for once
we're passing out inside the sleeping mausoleum

This is my safe house in the hurricane
here is where my love lays
200 treasured bones
this is my warmth behind the cold war
that day is what I'm living for
forever coming home

Here's to the room I can rest in
the door I'll always open
never to be closed
you as my horizon line
the star I navigate by
takes me back to hold 200 perfect bones

On absent days I will return to this place
and play a silent colour film within my head
in which the pillow leaves a code upon your face
and all at once it all makes perfect sense

400 bones, crumpled in bed
I'm the only one who knows that you're still breathing.

~~LUMP STREET SAFETY~~

LUMP STREET

HE'S A FULL GROWN MAN
NO SHOULDER TO CRY ON
RAISED BY WOLVES
AND THEY TOLD HIM TO BITE

NO ~~X~~ LOCKS ON THE DOORS
~~NEVER~~ TO DIVE ~~IN~~ IN
SCARS LIKE ARMOUR
~~READY TO FIGHT FOR A LIGHT~~
EXPECTING TO ~~FIGHT~~ DIE

                    LUMP STREET
~~SHE'S A~~ ~~STREET LEAN~~ GIRL
WITH A BLADE IN HER BROW
~~HE~~ RAISED BY THE ~~STATE~~ SAME
                            STATE
~~RAISED BY THE~~
TORN BY ~~THE TOWN~~
~~BUT THE TORE HER DOWN~~
THAT TORE ~~HER DOWN~~ DOWN
               IT OU
KICKING ~~HER~~ ~~STONES~~ BONES
ON LUMP STREET
THE BROGUE DESIGNED TO ~~TELL~~
~~TO TELL~~ THE PALE-FACED LIE
~~NOT A CAREFUL~~ TONE
~~YOU'RE~~ ON LUMP STREET
THERE'S A
~~THE~~ BROKEN JAW BELOW
THAT A DOG-TOOTHED SMILE

RACKING UP
NOTHING GROWS
HERE ON LUMP STREET
EVERYTHING IS ~~FIRED~~ IN A
BROKEN MOULD

~~NOBODY KNOW~~
~~HOW THEY GOT HERE~~
GET TOGETHER NOW - FIND HOPE(
HAVE YOU SEEN ENOUGH
~~DO YOU WANNA LEAVE~~

"LUMP STREET"

In a commissioned town, on Lump Street
the brick-hard boy repeats a scripted lie
eyes to the ground on Lump Street
there's a broken jaw behind the dog-tooth smile

The grunt and moan behind the night here
though breath is warm, sex is cold
nothing is grown on Lump Street
each piece is fired inside a broken mould

Do you want more unshapely love?
What you waiting for? Cut out that lump

She tore his tongue out at the end of Lump Street
she liked to see the blood beneath his skin
he wore her muscles, kissed all of the bruising
away, away

Do you want more unshapely love?
What you waiting for? Cut out that lump

He's a full-grown man, no shoulder to cry on
raised by wolves and they taught him to bite down hard
no locks on the doors, no corner to hide in
scars like armour, dead boys eyes

She's a Lump Street girl, with a blade in her brow
raised by the state but they tore it all down
they fucked, and they fought but it still felt right
run away from these orange Lump Street lights

Get together now
find hope
there is a life beyond the one you already know
get together now
build a home
there is a life beyond the one you already know.

"DIE LIKE A RICH BOY"

I need to find somebody who can tear me away
from the car crime babies and switchblade days
the bark of the unemployment hounds
and the thud of the thick white skull on the ground
I won't die in the bony arms of the state
to be laid to rest in the wake of a faded town

If the raincoats come to steal my home
there's a big white house at the end of the road
I can see you wrapped in Egyptian thread
in a marble garden immune to the mess
if you leave this world in a rhinestone shroud
we could finally make your father proud

If I leave this world in a loaded daze
I can finally have and eat my cake

I wanna die like a rich boy, diving
in a hydrocodone dream
and you can die like a rich girl by me
oh, how the magazines will grieve
I'll die like a rich boy, bathing
in a milk bath I could drown
I wanna die like a rich boy, even if we're
as poor as we are now
I wanna die like a rich boy, drowning
in a lake that bears my name
and you can die like a rich girl by me
flushed and radiant with fame
I wanna lie in state on the TV
in a golden cardboard crown
I wanna die like a rich boy even if we're
as poor as we are now

I've found you now so tear me away
from the feral street they lumped us in
I'll be Shakespeare's moonstruck king
we can lose our minds at the top of the hill
we burn cash and carry a decadent flame
way into the night and beyond the grave.

"THE WRECK"

Come out from under our covers
put on your clothes
we're both sinking tonight
wherever it goes

After somebody hammers
emergency glass
sing in key with the sirens
you're so bad

As the saltwater gushes
into our ship's holes
don't you dare jump without me
I'm not good on my own

You're not leaving this wreck
we're both going down with it

There is peace beyond trouble
and I'm desperate to meet you
below the blue surface
in a quiet reprieve

We're too poor to be precious
so cut off your nose and
come dying with me darling
the bed of the ocean's

Great tank of disaster
it wrecks who it pleases
the swell pulls me under
come under with me

You're not leaving this wreck
we're both going down with it
you're not leaving this wreck
we're both going down with it
you're not leaving this wreck
I've got pills in my pocket.

"WAIT 'TIL THE MORNING"

On the ugly side of midnight without a script
the mask has slipped
and make-up runs in mirrors down the stair
it's the usual case of
the only point being proven
is the one that was first made

Wait 'til the morning
the hours will turn you as you lay
wait 'til the morning
when no one's listening anyway
no greater good will come of it
just wait...

When eyes are bloodshot tired it's time to make
a swift escape and stop
trying to change a shovel into a spade
it's all the same
but the evening lacks the foresight to concede
and no one sees
the names upon the leaderboard
'cause no one's in the lead

So wait 'til the morning
the hours will turn you as you sleep
wait 'til the morning
burn the fiendish effigy
throw out the lofty arguments
there are no more ways to say these things
we are all designed to wax and wane
the light will come back on again
just wait...
just wait

Wait 'til the morning
wait 'til the morning.

618-16151161/148

"A LICK OF PAINT"

I know you're listening
I know you're there
I'll cut the dick act
pull up a chair

We get listless
and worn with age
I can see it now
there's a crack in the paint

There's no shame in
shutting down
but we could say more
and think aloud

It wasn't you
it didn't break
but we could use
a lick of paint

Remember Idaho
with nothing to do?
It can get like that
sometimes it should

There's medication
that we can take
but they kill our judgement
and strip the paint

There is time
so take some rest
don't worry too much
it can be repaired

It could be me
who's to blame
I think I need
a lick of paint.

REF   618-1819.

ARTIST
        FRIGHTENED RABBIT

TITLE
        "Recorded Songs"

MONTH / YEAR

            SEPT **1 5 2017**

"ROADLESS"

I turned off the road
because I was bored
because I was empty
and we all need filling up
I'd been running on petrol fumes
and enough was not enough
so I walked, heel to my toes
on the wire between carefree
and not caring at all

I will go wherever I can
roadless as I am
roadless soul

I got lost
just hanging around
in a blur of the days and weeks and months
took the calendar down
and watched everyone going somewhere
while I waited to be found
at the cat piss inn
bathing in bleach
I'm too neutral now to find colour for my cheeks

I'll go wherever I can
roadless as I am
roadless soul

I'll go wherever I can
roadless as I am
oh, what a roadless soul.

"HOW IT GETS IN"

(with Julien Baker)

Bring all the bandages, pressure the wound
it's a bright, bright red that colours us in
good for the invalids, downers, and killers
in sick, sick beds and silicone drips

Buzzing towards me, spirit awakens
A once lived glitch and that's how it gets in

It's how it gets in, it's how it gets in
we're invisible lovers
Sister let me in
it's how it gets in, it's how it gets in
two invisible lovers
Sister let me in

Cowering youngsters, elastic and covered
in feather-down hair all standing on end
even the others thick skin bears the evidence
cuts so thin, how does it get in?
How does it get in?
There's a place where you live

It's how it gets in, it's how it gets in
we're invisible lovers
Sister let me in
it's how it gets in, it's how it gets in
two invisible lovers
Sister let me in

it's how it gets in, it's how it gets in
two invisible lovers

Opened by instruments, closed by a thread
there's a space in the stitch.

618-1819/02

"RAINED ON"

I've been living in a dustbowl with half closed eyes
and if I believe the radio the levy is dry
there is sick on the pavement from seven weeks ago
nothing is sacred, not even our home
feels like there's a drug dust filling up my nose

I won't be sorry anymore
since January 1st
when everything got rained on
washed away the dirt
saw the heavens letting go
in a melancholy burst
everything got rained on
didn't even hurt

Everything has changed, not for better or for worse

Are they tears or is it rain?
Doesn't matter anymore
in the end they're both the same
we're less filthy than before
didn't ask for a downpour
didn't need a flood
Still, I think I found the answer
somewhere in the mud

All this lying in the sun doesn't fill my cup

I won't be sorry anymore
since January 1st
when everything got rained on
washed away the dirt
saw the heavens letting go
in a melancholy burst
everything got rained on
didn't even hurt

I don't plan on feeling empty for any longer than I must
if California needs a drink, I'll be joining her for one.

"CREDITS"

618-3185492019

"Wedding Gloves"
Lyrics by Scott Hutchison and Aidan Moffat
Music by Frightened Rabbit
© 2012 Domino Publishing Company Ltd.
All Rights Reserved

Handwritten text and illustrations by Scott Hutchison
Designed and typeset by DLT
Edited by Lucy Holliday
Printed and bound in Turkey by Imago

ISBN: 0-571-54241-7
EAN: 978-0-571-54241-3
Reproducing this book in any form is illegal and
forbidden by the Copyright, Designs and Patents Act, 1988

To buy Faber Music publications or to find out about the
full range of titles available please contact your local
retailer or Faber Music sales enquiries:

Faber Music Limited, Burnt Mill, Elizabeth Way,
Harlow, CM20 2HX, England
Tel: +44 (0) 1279 82 89 82
fabermusic.com

APPENDIX "A"

I left 'Howse' without a fucking clue,
left New York City, girl, without you.
But the sun does shine in this place some days,
and even when there's cloud there isn't always rain.

I'll stow away my greys
in a padlocked case, in a padlocked room.
Only to be released
when I sing all the songs I wrote about you.
This is the last one that I'll do.

Now I'm free in parentheses,
I'm not sure what I ought to do with it.
It sits in the house bright eyes and raised hand,
if I ignore its advances then the hand goes down.

I'll stow away my greys,
in a padlocked case & in a padlocked room.
Only to be released
when I sing all the songs I wrote about you.
This is the last one that I'll do.

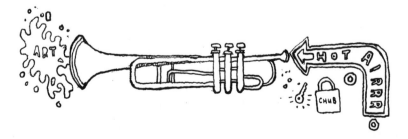

I FEEL BETTER

AND BETTER

AND WORSE & THEN BETTER

THAN EVER

THAN EVER

THAN EVER

I FEEL MUCH BETTER

AND BETTER

AND WORSE & THEN BETTER

THAN EVER

THAN EVER

THAN EVER

THAN EVER

I'll stow away my greys
in a padlocked case & in a padlocked room.
Only to be released
when I see you walking 'round with someone new
This is the last song, this is the last song
this is the last song I'll write about you.

FOOTNOTE - THIS IS A BLATANT LIE.

APPENDIX "B"

Tiny Changes is a mental health charity with a focus on helping and supporting children and young people tackle the ever growing challenges they face growing up.

We support worthwhile projects from money raised, we ask people to tell their stories as we have told ours, and we are pushing the boundaries to raise awareness of what needs to be done to make things better.

We will be hopeful and brave when faced with challenges, and we will be honest and kind in how we communicate.

We are determined to make an impact, and at the core of what we do is listening to the needs of young people.

Together, we are making a difference.

Together, we'll make tiny changes to earth.

www.tinychanges.com

And while I'm alive
I'll make tiny changes
to earth.

LIVER   LUNG   FR

⬭   🫁   ♡